CROCHET FLOWER

SQUARES & MOTIFS

30 crochet patterns for flower designs inspired by decorative tiles

EDITED BY SARAH CALLARD

DAVID & CHARLES
—PUBLISHING—

www.davidandcharles.com

CONTENTS

HOW TO USE THIS BOOK

This collection of flower designs features patterns inspired by decorative ceramic tiles from around the world. Each pattern has a chart, either a stitch chart – which also shows the colour of each stitch – or a colour chart showing colour changes for tiles made using the tapestry technique.

You can work from the stitch charts instead of the written pattern, but since the colour charts do not show which stitch is being worked you will also need to follow the pattern. Some of the colour charts only show one segment of the design, so will need to be repeated several times around to make the complete design.

BASIC KIT

All you will need for these patterns is a crochet hook and some yarn, plus a yarn needle for weaving in ends or invisible joins. Most only need small amounts of each colour, so they are a great stash-buster. The projects specify the yarn amounts needed, and any other supplies required to complete the item.

US/UK TERMINOLOGY

All the patterns are written using US crochet terms. See the table below for the equivalent UK stitch names.

US TERM	UK TERM
single crochet	double crochet
half double crochet	half treble
double crochet	treble crochet
treble crochet	double treble
double treble crochet	triple teble crochet

GAUGE (TENSION)

This is not critical on these blocks, but the patterns do give the ideal size of the tile. If your tiles are working up smaller, try a larger size hook than stated. If larger, try a smaller hook.

ABBREVIATIONS

approx, approximately
beg, beginning
BLO, back loop only
BPdc, back post double crochet
BPhdc, back post half double
BPsc, back post single crochet
ch, chain
ch-sp, chain space
cont, continue(d)
dc, double crochet
dc2tog, double crochet 2 stitches together
dc3tog, double crochet 3 stitches together
dc4tog, double crochet 4 stitches together
dtr, double treble crochet
FPdc, front post double crochet
FPhdc, front post half double crochet
FPsc, front post single crochet
FPtr, front post treble
FLO, front loop only
foll, follow(ing)
hdc, half double crochet
prev, previous
rep, repeat
RS, right side
sc, single crochet
sc2tog, single crochet 2 stitches together
sc3tog, single crochet 3 stitches together
skip, miss
slst, slip stitch
sp, space
st(s), stitch(es)
stsc, standing single crochet
stdc, standing double crochet
sthdc, standing half double crochet
sttr, standing treble
tr, treble crochet
tr3tog, treble 3 stitches together
tr4tog, treble 4 stitches together
WS, wrong side
yoh, yarn over hook
* – repeat instructions following asterisk as directed
[ ] – work instructions within brackets as many times stated

CROCHET CHART SYMBOLS

Symbol	Name		Symbol	Name		Symbol	Name
⬭	chain		dc4tog			4dc-PC	
•	slip stitch		tr3tog			5dc-PC	
+	single crochet		tr4tog			2ch-picot	
T	half double crochet		2dc-cl			3ch-picot	
⊤	double crochet		3dc-cl			4hdc-puff st	
⊤	treble crochet		4dc-cl			spike sc	
⊤	double treble crochet		2tr-cl			spike hdc	
⌣	front loop		3tr-cl			spike dc	
⌢	back loop		4tr-cl			V-st	
ʀ	third loop		5tr-cl			W-st	
↺	front post		2dtr-cl				
↻	back post		2dc-bobble				
⋏	sc2tog		3dc-bobble				
⋏	sc3tog		4dc-bobble				
⋏	dc2tog		5dc-bobble				
⋏	dc3tog		4tr-bobble				
			3dc-PC				

SPRING GARDEN

DESIGNER: ANA MORAIS SOARES

YARN

Rosários4 Regata, light worsted (DK), in foll shades:
Colour 1: Green (27)
Colour 2: White Pearl (01)
Colour 3: Pale Lilac (68)
Colour 4: Pink (45)

HOOK

US size E/4 (3.5mm) hook

GAUGE (TENSION)

A single motif measures approx 7in (18cm) using a US size E/4 (3.5mm) hook.

SPECIAL ABBREVIATIONS

3dc-cl, cluster of 3 dc
4dc-cl, cluster of 4 dc
3tr-cl, cluster of 3 tr
2dtr-cl, cluster of 2 dtr

PATTERN

Using E/4 hook and colour 1, make a magic ring.

Round 1: 1 ch (does not count as st throughout), 8 sc in ring, slst in first sc to join. (8 sc)

Round 2: 1 ch, 1 sc in same st, [4 ch, 1 sc in next st] 7 times, 4 ch, slst in first sc to join. (8 sc, 8 x 4ch-sp)

Fasten off colour 1.

Round 3: Join colour 2, [1 hdc in 4ch-sp, 4 ch] 8 times, slst in first hdc to join. (8 hdc, 8 x 4ch-sp)

Fasten off colour 2.

Round 4: Join colour 3, [4dc-cl in 4ch-sp, 5 ch] 8 times, slst in first 4dc-cl to join. (8 clusters, 8 x 5ch-sp)

Fasten off colour 3.

Round 5: Join colour 4, [1 FPhdc around 4dc-cl, 3 sc in 5ch-sp, 3tr-cl around hdc from Round 3 working in front of 5ch-sp, 3 sc in same 5ch-sp] 8 times, slst in first FPhdc to join. (8 clusters, 8 hdc, 48 sc)

Fasten off colour 4.

Round 6: Join colour 1, 1 scBLO in each st around, slst in first sc to join. (64 sc)

Fasten off colour 1.

Round 7: Join colour 2, *(1 dc, 2 ch, 1 tr, 2 ch, 1 dc) in sc worked in a 3tr-cl from Round 5 (first corner made), 3 ch, skip next 3 sts, 1 hdc in next st, 3 ch, skip next 3 sts, 1 sc in next st, 3 ch, skip next 3 sts, 1 hdc in next st, 3 ch, skip next 3 sts; rep from * 3 more times, slst in first dc to join. (4 tr, 8 dc, 8 hdc, 4 sc, 16 x 3ch-sp, 8 x 2ch-sp)

Round 8: 1 ch, 1 FPhdc around same st, 2 hdc in next 2ch-sp, *(1 FPdc, 2 ch, 1 FPdc) around next st (corner made), 2 hdc in next 2ch-sp, 1 FPhdc around next st, [3 hdc in next 3ch-sp, 1 FPhdc around next st] 4 times, 2 hdc in next 2ch-sp; rep from * 3 more times omitting last FPhdc and 2 hdc, slst in first FPhdc to join. (8 FPdc, 20 FPhdc, 64 hdc, 4 x 2ch-sp corners)

Fasten off colour 2.

Round 9: Join colour 1, *(1 hdc, 2 ch, 1 hdc) in 2ch-sp corner, 23 hdc; rep from * 3 more times, slst in first hdc to join. (100 hdc, 4 x 2ch-sp corners)

Fasten off colour 1.

Round 10: Join colour 2, working entire round in 3rd loop of hdc from prev round (loop behind "v" of st), *(2 hdc, 2 ch, 2 hdc) in 2ch-sp corner, 25 hdc; rep from * 3 more times, slst in first hdc to join. (116 hdc, 4 x 2ch-sp corners)

Fasten off colour 2.

Round 11: Join colour 4, working entire round in 3rd loop of hdc from prev round, *(2 hdc, 2 ch, 2 hdc) in 2ch-sp corner, 29 hdc; rep from * 3 more times, slst in first hdc to join. (132 hdc, 4 x 2ch-sp corners)

Fasten off colour 4.

Round 12: Join colour 3, *(3dc-cl, 4 ch, 3dc-cl) in 2ch-sp corner, skip first st, [2 ch, skip 2 sts, 3dc-cl in next st] 10 times, 2 ch, skip 2 last sts; rep from * 3 more times, slst in first 3dc-cl to join. (48 clusters, 44 x 2ch-sp, 4 x 4ch-sp corners)

Fasten off colour 3.

Round 13: Join colour 1, *(3 hdc, 2dtr-cl in 2ch-sp from Round 11 working between 3dc-cl already made there and in front of 4ch-sp, 3 hdc) in 4ch-sp corner, [1 FPhdc around next st, 2 hdc in 2ch-sp] 11 times, 1 FPhdc around next st; rep from * 3 more times, slst in first hdc to join. (4 x 2dtr-cl, 48 FPhdc, 112 hdc, 4 x 2dtr-cl corners)

Fasten off colour 1.

Round 14: Join colour 2, working entire round in 3rd loop of hdc from prev round, *(1 FPhdc, 2 ch, 1 FPhdc) around 2dtr-cl, 40 hdc; rep from * 3 more times, slst in first FPhdc to join. (8 FPhdc, 160 hdc, 4 x 2ch-sp corners)

Fasten off colour 2.

Round 15: Join colour 4, *3 sc in 2ch-sp corner, slstBLO in each st around; rep from * 3 more times, slst in first sc to join. (168 slsts, 4 x 3-sc corners)

Fasten off and weave in ends.

BLUE HYGGE

DESIGNER: CAITIE MOORE

YARN

Nurturing Fibres Eco-Cotton, light worsted (DK), in foll shades:
Colour 1: Pecan
Colour 2: Vanilla
Colour 3: Old Gold
Colour 4: Denim
Colour 5: Watershed

HOOK

US size G/6 (4mm) hook

OTHER TOOLS AND MATERIALS

4 stitch markers

GAUGE (TENSION)

A single motif measures approx 6in (15cm) using a US size G/6 (4mm) hook.

SPECIAL ABBREVIATION

2ch-picot, picot with 2 ch

NOTE

Join yarn with standing sts unless otherwise indicated, and join round with invisible join in standing st.

PATTERN

Using G/6 hook and colour 1, make a magic ring.

Round 1: 2 ch (counts as 1 hdc), 7 hdc, pull on tail to close ring. (8 hdc)

Fasten off colour 1.

Round 2: Join colour 2 in any st, 1 sc in each st around. (8 sc)

Fasten off colour 2.

Round 3: Join colour 3 in any st, *(1 scFLO, 1 hdcFLO, 1 dcFLO, 2ch-picot, 1 dcFLO, 1 hdcFLO, 1 scFLO) in same st (petal made), slst in next st; rep from * to end. (4 petals, 4 picot)

Fasten off colour 3.

Round 4 (WS): Join colour 4 in any BLO from Round 2, *(1 hdcBLO, 1 ch, 1 hdcBO) in same st; rep from * to end. (24 sts)

Fasten off colour 4.

Round 5 (RS): Join colour 4 in any 1ch-sp, *(1 sc, 1 hdc, 1 dc, 2ch-picot, 1 dc, 1 hdc, 1 sc) in 1ch-sp (petal made), skip next st, slst in next st; rep from * to end. (8 petals, 8 picot)

continued on next page >

Fasten off colour 4.

Round 6 (WS): Join colour 5 in any hdc from Round 4, *1 FPdc around hdc, 1 ch; rep from * to end. (16 dc, 16 ch)

Fasten off colour 5.

Round 7 (RS): Join colour 5 in 1ch-sp aligned between petals from Round 5, *(2 hdc, 1 dc, 2ch-picot, 1 dc, 2 hdc) in 1ch-sp (petal made), 1 sc in next hdc, 1 sc in 1ch-sp, 1 sc in next hdc; rep from * to end. (8 petals, 8 picot)

Fasten off colour 5.

Round 8 (WS): Join colour 4 in any FPdc from Round 6, *1 FPdc around FPdc, 1 ch; rep from * to end. (16 dc, 16 ch)

Fasten off colour 4.

Round 9 (RS): Join colour 4 in any 1ch-sp aligned between two petals from Round 7, *(2 hdc, 1 dc, 2ch-picot, 1 dc, 2 hdc) in 1ch-sp (petal made), 1 sc in next hdc, 1 sc in 1ch-sp, 1 sc in next hdc; rep from * to end. (8 petals, 8 picot)

Fasten off colour 4.

Round 10 (WS): Join colour 5 in any FPdc from Round 6, *1 FPdc around FPdc, 2 ch; rep from * to end. (16 dc, 16 x 2ch-sp)

Fasten off colour 5.

Round 11 (RS): Join colour 5 in 2ch-sp aligned between two petals from Round 9, *(2 hdc, 1 dc, 2ch-picot, 1 dc, 2 hdc) in 2ch-sp (petal made), 1 sc in next hdc, 1 sc in 2ch-sp, 1 sc in next hdc; rep from * to end. (8 petals, 8 picot)

Fasten off colour 5.

Round 12: Join colour 1 in first dc to left of any picot, *9 scBLO, 1 ch, skip picot; rep from * to end. (72 sc, 8 ch)

Fasten off colour 1.

Round 13: Join colour 2 in any 1ch-sp, *1 sc in 1ch-sp, 3 scBLO, 3 hdcBLO, 3 scBLO; rep from * to end. (56 sc, 24 hdc)

Fasten off colour 2.

Round 14: Join colour 2 in any st, 1 sc in each around. (80 sc)

Fasten off colour 2.

Round 15: Join colour 3 in any st, 1 hdcBLO in each st around. (80 hdc)

Fasten off colour 3.

Line up motif so petals from Round 1 are in north, south, east and west positions. Clockwise from top, these are petals 1, 2, 3 and 4. Place st marker in hdc (from prev round) directly above petal from Round 9 that lies between petal 1 and petal 2. Count 19 sts (excluding one with marker) and place another marker in next st. This st should be above a petal that lies between petal 2 and 3. Rep around to mark out 4 corners.

Round 16: Join colour 4 at any st marker, *(1 tr, 1 ch, 1 tr) in same st, 3 dcBLO, 3 hdcBLO, 7 scBLO, 3 hdcBLO, 3 dcBLO; rep from * to end. (84 sts, 4 x 1ch-sp corners)

Fasten off colour 4.

Round 17: Join colour 5 in any 1ch-sp, *(2 dc, 1 ch, 2 dc) in 1ch-sp, skip next st, 3 FPdc, 3 FPhdc, skip next st, 6 scBLO, 3 FPhdc, 3 FPdc; rep from * around. (88 sts, 4 ch)

Fasten off, remove st markers, and weave in ends.

ROUNDS 1-3

ROUNDS 4-5

ROUNDS 6-7

ROUNDS 8-9

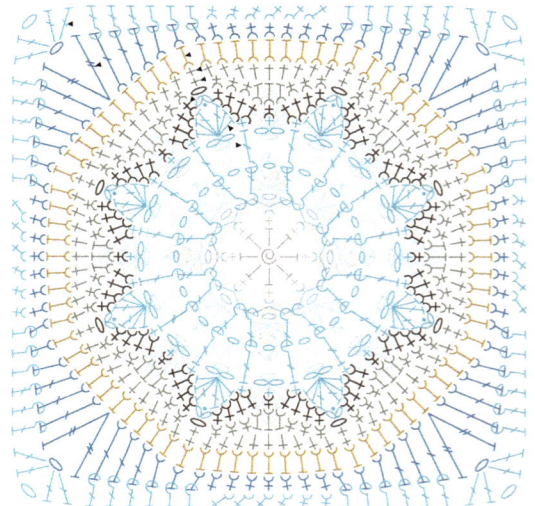

ROUNDS 10-17

ATHENA

DESIGNER: HATTIE RISDALE

YARN

Paintbox Yarns Cotton DK, light worsted (DK), in foll shades:

Colour 1: Marine Blue (434)
Colour 2: Candyfloss Pink (450)
Colour 3: Champagne White (403)
Colour 4: Washed Teal (433)

HOOK

US size G/6 (4mm) hook

GAUGE (TENSION)

A single motif measures approx 7in (18cm) using a US size G/6 (4mm) hook.

SPECIAL ABBREVIATION

3dc-cl, cluster of 3 dc

PATTERN

Using G/6 hook and colour 1, make a magic ring.

Round 1: Working in ring, 2 ch (counts as part of 3dc-cl), complete 3dc-cl, 2 ch, *3dc-cl, 2 ch; rep from * 4 more times, slst in top of beg 3dc-cl to join. (6 clusters, 6 x 2ch-sp)

Fasten off colour 1.

Round 2: Join colour 2 with slst in any 2ch-sp, 3 ch (counts as 1 dc throughout), 5 dc in same ch-sp, *skip cluster, 6 dc in next ch-sp; rep from * around, slst in 3rd of beg 3-ch to join. (36 dc)

Fasten off colour 2.

Round 3: Join colour 1 with slst in any sp between two 6-dc groups, 3 ch, *(1 dc, 4 ch, 1 dc) in middle of 6-dc group, 2 dc in sp between two 6-dc groups; rep from * 4 more times, (1 dc, 4 ch, 1 dc) in middle of 6-dc group, 1 dc in beg ch-sp, slst in 3rd of beg 3-ch to join. (24 dc, 6 x 4ch-sp)

Fasten off colour 1.

Round 4: Join colour 3 with slst between 2 dc, *1 ch, (4 dc, 2 ch, 4 dc, 1 ch) in 4ch-sp, slst between 2 dc; rep from * around, with final slst in beg slst to join. (48 dc, 12 ch-sp, 6 x 2ch-sp)

Fasten off colour 3.

Round 5: Join colour 1 with slst in any 2ch-sp (at tip of petal), 2 ch (counts as 1 sc, 1 ch), *(3 tr, 3 ch) in 1ch-sp (at base of petal), (3 tr, 1 ch) in next 1ch-sp (at base of next petal), (2 sc, 1 ch) in 2ch-sp (at tip of petal); rep from * 4 more times, (3 tr, 3 ch) in 1ch-sp, (3 tr, 1 ch) in next 1ch-sp, 1 sc in last 2ch-sp, slst in first of beg 2-ch to join. (36 tr, 12 sc, 12 ch, 6 x 3ch-sp corners)

Fasten off colour 1.

Round 6: Join colour 2 with slst in any 1ch-sp to right of 2-sc, 2 ch (counts as 1 hdc thoughout), (2 hdc, 1 ch) in same sp, (3 hdc, 1 ch) in next 1ch-sp, *(3 hdc, 1 ch, 3 hdc, 1 ch) in 3ch-sp, (3 hdc, 1 ch) in next two 1ch-sps; rep from * 4 more times, (3 hdc, 1 ch, 3 hdc, 1 ch) in final 3ch-sp, slst in 2nd of beg 2-ch. (72 hdc, 24 ch)

Fasten off colour 2.

Round 7: Join colour 4 with slst in any 1ch-sp to left of corner group, 2 ch, (2 hdc, 1 ch) in same sp, (3 hdc, 1 ch) in next two ch-sps, (2 hdc, 1 ch, 2 hdc, 1 ch) in corner sp, *(3 hdc, 1 ch) in next three ch-sps, (2 hdc, 1 ch, 2 hdc, 1 ch) in corner sp; rep from * 4 more times, slst in 2nd of beg 2-ch to join. (78 hdc, 30 ch)

Fasten off colour 4.

Round 8: Join colour 3 with slst in any 1ch-sp to left of corner, 3 ch, 2 dc in same sp, *4 dc in next two ch-sps, 3 dc in next sp, (2 dc, 2 ch, 2 dc) in corner sp; rep from * around, slst in 3rd of beg 3-ch to join. (108 dc, 6 x 2ch-sp corners)

Fasten off and weave in ends.

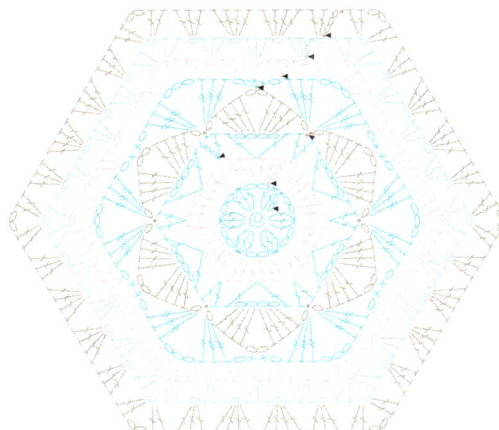

LACEFLOWER

DESIGNER: RACHELE CARMONA

YARN

Scheepjes Softfun, light worsted (DK), in foll shade:
Lace (2426)

HOOK

US size G/6 (4mm) hook

GAUGE (TENSION)

A single motif measures approx 6in (15cm) using a US size G/6 (4mm) hook.

SPECIAL ABBREVIATIONS

2dc-cl, cluster of 2 dc
3dc-cl, cluster of 3 dc
3tr-cl, cluster of 3 tr

PATTERN

Using G/6 hook, 3 ch, slst to join into a ring.

Round 1: (1 sc, 2 ch) in ring (counts as first tr), [1 ch, 1 tr in ring] 11 times, 1 ch, slst in first tr to join. (12 tr, 12 ch)

Round 2: (1 sc, 1 ch, 2dc-cl) all in first ch-sp (counts as first 3dc-cl), [3 ch, 3dc-cl in next ch-sp] 11 times, 3 ch, slst in first 3dc-cl to join. (12 x 3dc-cl, 12 x 3ch-sp)

Round 3: 4 sc in each ch-sp, slst in first sc to join. (48 sc)

Round 4: 1 sc in next st, [3 ch, skip 1 st, 1 sc in next st] 23 times, 3 ch, slst in first sc to join. (24 sc, 24 x 3ch-sp)

Round 5: Slst in first ch, 1 sc in 3ch-sp, *5 ch, [3tr-cl in next 3ch-sp, 2 ch] 4 times, 3tr-cl in next 3ch-sp, 5 ch, 1 sc in next 3ch-sp; rep from * 3 more times omitting final sc, slst in first sc to join. (20 x 3tr-cl, 4 sc, 16 x 2ch-sp, 8 x 5ch-sp)

Round 6: Slst in first 3 ch, 1 sc in 5ch-sp, *[3 ch, 1 sc in next 2ch-sp] 4 times, 3 ch, 1 sc in 5ch-sp, 5 ch, 1 sc in next 5ch-sp; rep from * 3 more times omitting final sc, slst in first sc to join. (24 sc, 20 x 3ch-sp, 4 x 5ch-sp)

Fasten off and weave in ends.

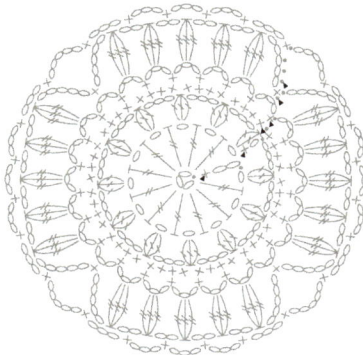

ESTRELLA

DESIGNER: JULIE YEAGER

YARN

Scheepjes Stone Washed, sport (4ply), in foll shades:
Colour 1: Pink Quartzite (821)
Colour 3: Peridot (827)
Scheepjes River Washed, sport (4ply), in foll shades:
Colour 2: Danube (948)
Colour 4: Rhine (952)

HOOK

US size G/6 (4mm)

GAUGE (TENSION)

A single motif measures approx 8in (20cm) using a US size G/6 (4mm) hook.

SPECIAL ABBREVIATIONS

2dc-cl, cluster of 2 dc
2dc-cl 3-group, ([2dc-cl, 2 ch] twice, 2dc-cl) in same sp
2dc-cl 5-group, ([2dc-cl, 2 ch] 4 times, 2dc-cl) in same sp

NOTES

When skipping sts, each ch counts as one stitch, and each cluster also counts as one stitch. First few rounds quickly alternate from square to diamond to square so corners are transient and can be 1ch-sp, 2ch-sp, 3ch-sp or 4ch-sp. To join with single crochet, yoh, insert in designated st, yoh and pull through (2 loops on hook), yoh and pull through both loops.

PATTERN

Using G/6 hook and colour 1, 5 ch, slst to join into a ring.

Round 1: 2 ch (counts as 1 hdc throughout), 1 dc in same sp to complete first 2dc-cl, 1 ch, 2dc-cl, [4 ch, 2dc-cl, 1 ch, 2dc-cl] 3 times, 4 ch, slst in top of 2dc-cl to join. (8 x 2dc-cl, 4 ch, 4 x 4ch-sp)

Fasten off colour 1.

Round 2: Join colour 2 with sc in any 4ch-sp, 4 sc in same sp, [1 FPsc around top of 2dc-cl, 1 ch, skip 1 ch, 1 FPsc around top of 2dc-cl, 5 sc in 4ch-sp] 4 times omitting last 5 sts, slst in first sc to join. (28 sc, 4 ch)

Fasten off colour 2.

Round 3: Join colour 3 with slst in 3rd sc of any 5-sc group, 2 ch, (1 dc, 1 ch, 1 dc, 1 hdc) in same st, [1 hdc, 1 sc, skip next st, (1 sc, 2 ch, 1 sc) in ch-sp, skip 1 st, 1 sc, 1 hdc, (1 hdc, 1 dc, 1 ch, 1 dc, 1 hdc) in next st] 4 times omitting last 5 sts, slst in top of beg 2-ch to join. (40 sts)

Fasten off colour 3.

Round 4: Join colour 4 with sc in any 1ch-sp, (2 ch, 1 sc) in same sp, [1 sc in dc, skip 3 sts, 2dc-cl, 1 ch, (2dc-cl, 3 ch, 2dc-cl) in 2ch-sp, 1 ch, 2dc-cl, skip 3 sts, 1 sc in dc, (1 sc, 2 ch, 1 sc) in 1ch-sp] 4 times omitting last 4 sts, slst in beg sc to join. (16 x 2dc-cl, 16 sc, 4 x 3ch-sp, 4 x 2ch-sp, 8 ch)

Fasten off colour 4.

Round 5: In this round sc to work into right after 2dc-cl 5-group is somewhat hidden. Join colour 1 with slst in any 2ch-sp, (2 ch, 1 dc in same st to complete first 2dc-cl, [2 ch, 2dc-cl] 4 times) in same sp for corner, [1 ch, 2dc-cl in next st, skip 2 sts, 1 sc in 1ch-sp, skip cluster, (1 sc, 2 ch, 1 sc) in 3-ch sp, skip cluster, 1 sc in 1ch-sp, skip 2 sts, 2dc-cl in next st, 1 ch, 2dc-cl 5-group in next 2ch-sp] 4 times omitting last 2dc-cl 5-group, slst in top of 2dc-cl to join. (4 x 2dc-cl 5-groups, 8 x 2dc-cl, 16 sc, 4 x 2ch-sp, 8 ch)

Fasten off colour 1.

Round 6: Join colour 3 with sc in first 2ch-sp of any 2dc-cl 5-group, 1 sc in same sp, 2 sc in next 2ch-sp, *2 ch, [2 sc in next 2ch-sp] twice, skip 4 sts, 2dc-cl in next st, 1 ch, 2dc-cl 5-group in 2ch-sp, 1 ch, 2dc-cl in next st, skip 4 sts, [2 sc in next 2ch-sp] twice; rep from * 3 more times omitting last 4 sts, slst in beg sc to join. (28 x 2dc-cl, 32 sc, 20 x 2ch-sp, 8 ch)

Fasten off colour 3.

Round 7: Join colour 4 with sc in first 2ch-sp of any 2dc-cl 5-group, 1 sc in same sp, 2 sc in next 2ch-sp, *2 ch for corner, [2 sc in next 2ch-sp] twice, skip cluster, 2dc-cl in 1ch-sp, skip 3 sts, [2dc-cl in next st] twice, 2dc-cl 5-group in 2ch-sp, [2dc-cl in next st] twice, skip 3 sts, 2dc-cl in 1ch-sp, skip cluster, [2 sc in next 2ch-sp] twice; rep from * 3 more times omitting last 4 sts, slst in beg sc to join. (44 x 2dc-cl, 32 sc, 20 x 2ch-sp)

Fasten off colour 4.

Round 8: Join colour 1 with slst in any corner 2ch-sp, (2 ch, 1 dc in same st to complete first 2dc-cl, [2 ch, 2dc-cl] 4 times) in same sp, [skip 5 sts, 2dc-cl 3-group in sp between clusters, 7 ch, skip 17 sts, 2dc-cl 3-group in sp between clusters, skip 5 sts, 2dc-cl 5-group in 2ch-sp] 4 times omitting last 2dc-cl 5-group, slst in top of beg 2dc-cl to join. (44 x 2dc-cl, 4 x 7ch-sp, 32 x 2ch-sp)

Fasten off colour 1. Push 7-ch "bridges" to back of work.

continued on next page >

ROUNDS 1-8

Round 9: Sc in this round are worked in 2ch-sp and around 7-ch bridge of Round 8. Join colour 3 with sc in first 2ch-sp of any 2dc-cl 5-group of Round 8, 1 sc in same sp, 2 sc in next 2ch-sp, *2 ch, [2 sc in next 2ch-sp] 4 times, 4 ch, 1 sc around 7-ch bridge, 4 ch, [2 sc in next 2ch-sp] 4 times; rep from * 3 more times omitting last 4 sts, slst in beg sc to join. (68 sc, 8 x 4ch-sp, 4 x 2ch-sp)

Round 10: 3 ch (counts as 1 dc), 3 dc, *(2 dc, 2 ch, 2 dc) in 2ch-sp), 4 dc, 2 hdc, 2 sc, [2 sc in 2ch-sp of Round 7, picking up 4ch-sp of Round 9] 4 times, 2 sc, 2 hdc, 4 dc; rep from * 3 more times omitting last 4 sts, slst in top of beg 3-ch to join. (48 dc, 16 hdc, 48 sc, 4 x 2ch-sp corners)

Fasten off and weave in ends.

ROUNDS 9-10

WHEN FLOWERS GO BLUE

DESIGNER: ANA MORAIS SOARES

YARN

Rosários4 Belmonte, light worsted (DK), in foll shades:
Colour 1: Dark Blue (29)
Colour 2: White Pearl (21)
Colour 3: Light Blue (27)
Colour 4: Green (31)

HOOK

US size E/4 (3.5mm) hook

GAUGE (TENSION)

A single motif measures approx 7½in (19cm) using a US size E/4 (3.5mm) hook.

SPECIAL ABBREVIATION

5dc-bobble, bobble of 5 dc

NOTES

For neater work, change slst at end of rounds to invisible join. Bobbles worked in Round 12 are separated by lengths of ch. In Round 13 bobbles are brought to front and chain pushed to back and Round 13 sts are worked over chain.

PATTERN

Using E/4 hook and colour 1, make a magic ring.

Round 1: 3 ch (counts as 1 dc), 11 dc in ring, slst in top of beg 3-ch to join. (12 dc)

Fasten off colour 1.

Round 2: Join colour 2, *(1 dc, 5 ch, 1 dc) in any st (corner made), 2 FPdc; rep from * 3 more times, slst in first dc to join. (16 dc, 4 x 5ch-sp corners)

Fasten off colour 2.

Round 3: Join colour 3, *(5 dc, 2 ch, 5 dc) in 5ch-sp corner, 3 ch, skip next 4 sts; rep from * 3 more times, slst in first dc to join. (40 dc, 4 x 3ch-sp, 4 x 2ch-sp corners)

Fasten off colour 3.

Round 4: Join colour 4, *3 sc in 2ch-sp corner (corner made), 5 BPhdc, 1 FPtr around 2nd of pair of FPdc from Round 2 working in front of 3ch-sp from prev round, 2 ch, 1 FPtr around first of pair of FPdc from Round 2 working in front of 3ch-sp from prev round, 5 BPhdc; rep from * 3 more times, slst in first sc to join. (12 sc, 40 BPhdc, 8 FPtr, 4 x 2ch-sp, 4 x 3-sc corners)

Fasten off colour 4.

Round 5: Join colour 1, *3 hdc in middle sc of 3-sc corner (corner made), 6 hdc, 1 ch, skip next st (FPtr from prev round), 5dc-bobble in next 2ch-sp also catching 3ch-sp from Round 3, 1 ch, skip next st (FPtr from prev round), 6 hdc; rep from * 3 more times, slst in first hdc to join. (4 bobbles, 60 hdc, 8 ch, 4 x 3 hdc corners)

Fasten off colour 1.

Round 6: Join colour 2, *(2 hdc, 2 ch, 2 hdc) in middle hdc of 3-hdc corner (corner made), 7 BPhdc, 1 FPhdc around bobble, 7 BPhdc; rep from * 3 more times, slst in first hdc to join. (16 hdc, 56 BPhdc, 4 FPhdc, 4 x 2ch-sp corners)

Round 7: 2 ch (counts as 1 hdc), 1 hdc in next st, *(1 hdc, 2 ch, 1 hdc) in next 2ch-sp corner, 19 hdc; rep from * 3 more times omitting last 2 hdc, slst in top of beg 2-ch to join. (84 hdc, 4 x 2ch-sp corners)

Fasten off colour 2.

Round 8: Join colour 4, working entire round in 3rd loop of hdc from prev round (loop behind "v" of st), *(2 hdc, 2 ch, 2 hdc) in 2ch-sp corner, 21 hdc; rep from * 3 more times, slst in first hdc to join. (100 hdc, 4 x 2ch-sp corners)

Fasten off colour 4.

Round 9: Join colour 1, *(1 sc, 2 ch, 1 sc) in 2ch-sp corner, 25 scBLO; rep from * 3 more times, slst in first sc to join. (108 sc, 4 x 2ch-sp corners)

Fasten off colour 1.

Round 10: Join colour 3, *(1 sc, 2 ch, 1 sc) in 2ch-sp corner, 27 scBLO; rep from * 3 more times, slst in first sc to join. (116 sc, 4 x 2ch-sp corners)

Round 11: 1 ch (does not count as st), 1 sc in same st, *(1 sc, 2 ch, 1 sc) in next 2ch-sp corner, 29 sc; rep from * 3 more times omitting last sc, slst in first sc to join. (124 sc, 4 x 2ch-sp corners)

Fasten off colour 3.

Round 12: Join colour 1, *(1 sc, 2 ch, 1 sc) in 2ch-sp corner, 7 ch, skip next 7 sts, [5dc-bobble in next st, 7 ch, skip next 7 sts] 3 times; rep from * 3 more times, slst in first sc to join. (12 bobbles, 8 sc, 16 x 7ch-sp, 4 x 2ch-sp corners)

Fasten off colour 1.

Round 13: Join colour 3, working all hdc in skipped sts from Round 11 and in front of 7ch-sp to pull bobbles to front, *(1 sc, 2 ch, 1 sc) in 2ch-sp corner, skip first st (corner sc from prev round), 7 hdc, [1 FPsc around bobble, 7 hdc] 3 times, 1 sc in last st; rep from * 3 more times, slst in first sc to join. (112 hdc, 12 FPsc, 12 sc, 4 x 2ch-sp corners)

continued on next page >

Round 14: 1 ch (does not count as st), 1 sc in same st, *(1 sc, 2 ch, 1 sc) in next 2ch-sp corner, 34 sc; rep from * 3 more times omitting last sc, slst in first sc to join. (144 sc, 4 x 2ch-sp corners)

Fasten off colour 3.

Round 15: Join colour 1, *(1 sc, 1 dtr in 2ch-sp from Round 11 working between two sc already there, 1 sc) in 2ch-sp corner, 36 sc; rep from * 3 more times, slst in first sc to join. (152 sc, 4 x dtr corners)

Fasten off colour 1.

Round 16: Join colour 4, *(1 hdc, 2 ch, 1 hdc) in dtr from prev round, 38 hdcBLO; rep from * 3 more times, slst in first hdc to join. (160 hdc, 4 x 2ch-sp corners)

Fasten off colour 4.

Round 17: Join colour 1, *(1 sc, 1 hdc, 1 sc) in 2ch-sp corner, 40 scBLO; rep from * 3 more times, slst in first sc to join. (168 sc, 4 x hdc corners)

Fasten off and weave in ends.

ARTEMIS

DESIGNER: HATTIE RISDALE

YARN

Sirdar Happy Cotton DK, light worsted (DK), in foll shades:
Colour 1: Tea Time (751)
Colour 2: Dolly (761)

HOOK

US size G/6 (4mm) hook

GAUGE (TENSION)

A single motif measures approx 5in (12.5cm) using a US size G/6 (4mm) hook.

SPECIAL ABBREVIATION

2dc-cl, cluster of 2 dc

PATTERN

(make 4 motifs of Rounds 1 and 2)

Using G/6 hook and colour 1, make a magic ring.

Round 1: Working in ring, 2 ch (counts as first part of 2dc-cl), complete 2dc-cl, 2dc-cl, 2 ch, *[2dc-cl] twice, 2 ch; rep from * 2 more times, slst in top of 2-ch to join. (8 clusters, 4 x 2ch-sp)

Fasten off colour 1.

Round 2: Join colour 2 with a slst in any space between pair of clusters, *(4 dc, 2 ch, 4 dc) in 2ch-sp, slst between pair of clusters; rep from * 3 more times, slst in beg slst to join. (32 dc, 4 x 2ch-sp)

Fasten off colour 2.

JOIN MOTIFS

Take Motif 1, slst to join colour 1 between pair of clusters in Round 1, [slstBLO in next 4 dc, (2 sc, 2 ch, 2 sc) in 2ch-sp, slstBLO in next 4 dc, slst between pair of clusters in Round 1] 4 times omitting final slst in beg sp, slst in beg slst to join.

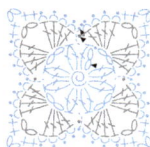

MOTIF

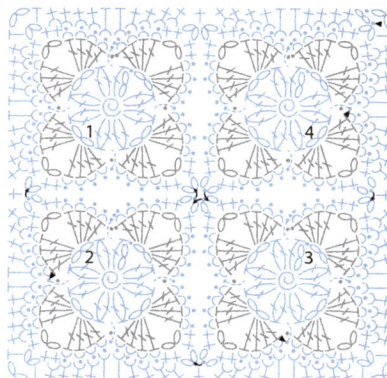

JOINING MOTIFS

Take Motif 2, slst to join colour 1 between 2 pairs of clusters in Round 1, rep section between [ ] twice, *slstBLO in next 4 dc, (2 sc, 1 ch, join to 2-ch sp in Motif 1 with slst, 1 ch, 2sc) in 2ch-sp, slstBLO in next 4dc, slst between two pairs of clusters in Round 1, rep from * joining to next 2ch-sp of Motif 1, omit final slst between two clusters, slst in beg sl st to join.

Take Motif 3, rep as for Motif 2, but join to Motif 2.

Take Motif 4, slst to join colour 1 between 2 pairs of clusters in Round 1, work section between [ ] once, slstBLO in next 4 dc, (2 sc, 1 ch, join to Motif 1 with slst, 1 ch, 2 sc) in 2ch-sp, slstBLO in next 4 dc, slst between 2 pairs of clusters of Round1, slstBLO in next 4 dc, (2 sc, 1 ch, join to Motif 1 with slst, join to Motif 3 with slst, 1 ch, 2 sc) in 2ch-sp, slstBLO in next 4 dc, slst between 2 pairs of clusters, slstBLO in next 4 dc, (2sc, 1ch, join to Motif 3 with slst, 1 ch, 2 sc) in 2ch-sp, slstBLO in next 4 dc, join to beg slst with a slst.

Fasten off colour 1.

BORDER

Join colour 1 with slst in any outside corner 2ch-sp, 2 ch (counts as 1 hdc), *[miss first sc, 4 scBLO, 1 hdcBLO, miss slst between petals, 1 hdcBLO, 4 scBLO], 1 sc in two corner sp, miss first sc, 4 scBLO, 1 hdcBLO, miss slst between petals, 1 hdcBLO, 4 scBLO, (1 hdc, 2 ch, 1 hdc) in corner 2 ch sp; rep from * 3 more times omitting final hdc, slst in 2nd ch of beg 2-ch to join. (68 sc, 24 hdc, 4 x 2ch-sp corners)

Fasten off and weave in ends.

ABSTRACT DAISY

DESIGNER: LYNNE ROWE

YARN

Scheepjes Stone Washed, sport (4ply), in foll shade:
Colour 1: Nile (944)
Scheepjes River Washed, sport (4ply), in foll shade:
Colour 2: Amazonite (813)

HOOK

US size E/4 (3.5mm) hook

GAUGE (TENSION)

A single motif measures approx 6½in (16.5cm) using a US size E/4 (3.5mm) hook

SPECIAL ABBREVIATIONS

sc/dc2tog, insert hook in next st, yoh, pull through, yoh, insert hook in next st, yoh, pull through, yoh, pull through first 2 loops, yoh, pull through all rem loops

dc/sc2tog, yoh, insert hook in next st, yoh, pull through, yoh, pull through first 2 loops, insert hook in next st, yoh, pull through, yoh and pull through all rem loops

NOTES

Motif is worked in tapestry crochet in rounds.
Change to next colour on last yoh of prev st. Carry unused yarn across work and crochet over, holding slightly to back of working st.
At beg of round (1 sc, 2 ch) replaces dc for neater st.

PATTERN

Change colour foll chart.

Using E/4 hook and colour 1, make a magic ring.

Round 1 (RS): 1 ch (does not count as st, throughout), 8 sc in ring, do not join round. (8 sc)

Round 2: 2 sc in each st, slst in first st to join. (16 sc)

Round 3: 1 ch, (1 sc, 2 ch, 1 dc) in same st, 1 dc, *2 dc in next st, 1 dc; rep from * to end, slst in top of 2-ch to join. (24 dc)

Round 4: 1 ch, (1 sc, 2 ch) in same st, 2 dc in next st, 2 dc in next st, *1 dc, 2 dc in next st, 2 dc in next st; rep from * to end, slst in top of 2-ch to join. (40 dc)

continued on next page >

Round 5: 1 ch, (1 sc, 2 ch, 1 dc) in same st, 1 dc, 2 dc in next st, 2 dc, *2 dc in next st, 1 dc, 2 dc in next st, 2 dc; rep from * to end, slst in top of 2-ch to join. (56 dc)

Round 6: 1 ch, starting in first st, *1 sc/dc2tog over next 2 sts, 1 dc, 1 dc/sc2tog over next 2 sts, 2 dc in next 2 sts; rep from * to end, slstBLO in first st to join. (56 dc)

Fasten off colour 1 and cont using colour 2 only.

Round 7: 1 ch, 1 scBLO in same st, 1 scBLO, *1 hdcBLO, 1 dc, (1 dc, 1 tr) in next st, 1 tr in sp before next st (for corner st), (1 tr, 1 dc) in next st, 1 dc, 1 hdcBLO, 2 scBLO, 4 sc, 2 scBLO; rep from * 3 times more omitting last 2 sts, slst in first sc to join. (68 sts)

Fasten off colour 2.

Round 8: Rejoin colour 2 in any corner st, 4 ch (counts as first tr), 2 tr in same st, *1 dc in each st to next corner st, 3 tr in corner st; rep from * to end omitting last corner, slst in top of beg 4-ch to join. (76 sts)

Fasten off colour 2.

Round 9: Join colour 1 in a corner st, 1 ch, *(2 sc, 1 dc, 2 sc) in same st, 1 sc in each st to next corner; rep from * to end, slst in top of first sc to join. (92 sts)

Fasten off colour 1, rejoin colour 2 in any corner st.

Round 10: As Round 8. (100 sts)

Fasten off colour 2, rejoin colour 1 in any corner st.

Round 11: As Round 8. (108 sts)

Fasten off and weave in ends.

KEY

■ Colour 1
■ Colour 2

Chart shows one side of square; it should be repeated four times on each round.

Read chart from bottom to top, right to left.

Each square represents one stitch.

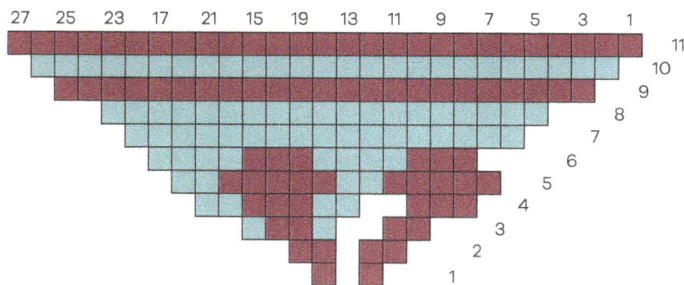

FRASERA

DESIGNER: CAITIE MOORE

YARN

Nurturing Fibres Eco-Cotton, light worsted (DK), in foll shades:

Colour 1: Watershed
Colour 2: Vanilla
Colour 3: Sunglow
Colour 4: Persian
Colour 5: Charcoal
Colour 6: Cobblestone

HOOK

US size G/6 (4mm) hook

GAUGE (TENSION)

A single motif measures approx 6in (15cm) using a US size G/6 (4mm) hook.

SPECIAL ABBREVIATIONS

5dc-PC, popcorn of 5 dc, 1 ch
4dc-PC, popcorn of 4 dc, 1 ch
2ch-picot, picot with 2 ch

NOTES

Join yarn with standing sts unless otherwise indicated, and join round with invisible join in standing st. When working in popcorn, always work in 1ch-sp at back.

PATTERN

Using G/6 hook and colour 1, make a magic ring.

Round 1: 6 sc, pull on tail to close ring. (6 sc)

Fasten off colour 1.

Round 2: Join colour 1 in front loop of any st, *(1 slstFLO, 1 ch, 1 hdcFLO, 1 ch, 1 slstFLO) in same st; rep from * around. (18 sts, 12 ch)

Fasten off colour 1.

Round 3: Join colour 1 in back loop from Round 1, 2 sc in each st. (12 sc)

Fasten off colour 1.

Round 4: Join colour 1 in front loops from Round 3, *(1 slstFLO, 1 ch, 1 hdcFLO, 1 ch, 1 slstFLO) in same st; rep from * around. (36 sts, 24 ch)

Fasten off colour 1.

Round 5: Join colour 1 in back loops from Round 3, *1 sc, 2 sc in same st; rep from * to end. (18 sc)

Fasten off colour 1.

Round 6: Join colour 1 in any st, *2 hdc, 2 hdc in same st; rep from * to end. (24 hdc)

Fasten off colour 1.

Round 7: Join colour 2 in any st through back loop and 3rd loop and work entire round this way, *1 hdc, 2 hdc in same st; rep from * to end. (36 hdc)

Fasten off colour 2.

Round 8: Join colour 3 in any st through back loop and 3rd loop and work entire round this way, *1 sc, 5dc-PC, 1 sc, 5dc-PC, 1 sc, 5 ch, skip 4 sts; rep from * to end. (12 sc, 8 PC, 4 x 5ch-sp)

Fasten off colour 3.

Round 9: Join colour 2 in front loop from Round 7 (in front of sc in back loop) immediately to right of first PC, *1 sc, 1 ch, 1 hdc in PC, 3 hdc in sc between two PCs, 1 hdc in PC, 1 ch, 1 scFLO in next sc in Round 7, cont working in Round 7, 4 hdc; rep from * to end. (44 sts, 8 ch)

Fasten off colour 2.

Round 10: Join colour 3 in 1 ch-sp to right of first PC, *1 slst, 1 ch, skip next hdc, 1 sc in first hdc of 3-hdc group, 5dc-PC, 1 sc, 1 ch, skip next hdc, 1 slst in 1ch-sp, 5 ch; rep from * to end. (4 PC, 8 sc, 8 slsts, 8 ch, 4 x 5ch-sp)

Fasten off colour 3.

Round 11: Join colour 2 to Round 9 in 1ch-sp to right of PC from prev round, *2 sc in Round 9 1ch-sp (working over slst from Round 9), 3 dc in first hdc of group from Round 9 (working over sc from prev round), (2 dc, 1 ch, 2 dc) in PC, 3 dc in 3rd hdc of group from Round 9 (working over sc from prev round), 2 sc in Round 9 1ch-sp (working over slst from Round 9), 7 sc in 6ch-sp; rep from * to end. (84 sts, 4 ch)

Fasten off colour 2.

Round 12: Join colour 4 in first of 7-sc (worked in 6ch-sp in prev round), *1 sc, 1 FPdc around first hdc from Round 9 below, 1 FPdc around next hdc, skip 2 sts in Round 11, 1 sc, without skipping any sts in Round 9, 2 FPdc, skip 2 sts in Round 11, 1 sc, 8 ch behind petal; rep from * to end. (28 sts, 4 x 8ch-sp)

Fasten off colour 4.

Round 13: Join colour 2 to Round 9 in sc to right of pair of PC, *1 dc, now work in Round 11 around petal, 1 sc in sc, 6 hdc, (2 dc, 2ch-picot, 2 dc) in 1ch-sp, 6 hdc, 1 sc, 1 dc in round 9, skip Round 12 sc and cont in Round 11, 2 hdc, skip next st, 2 hdc, skip next st; rep from * to end. (96 sts, 4 picot)

Fasten off colour 2.

Round 14: Join colour 4 to Round 12 and work only in Round 12, *1 slst in first sc after 8-ch behind Round 13, 2 FPdc around FPdcs, skip 1 sc, 2 FPdc around FPdcs, 1 slst in sc, 8 ch behind petal; rep from * to end. Do not fasten off. (24 sts, 4 x 8ch-sp)

continued on next page >

Round 15: Cont with colour 4, *1 slst in slst after 8-ch from prev round, 4dc-PC in each FPdc, 1 slst, 8 ch behind petal; rep from * to end. (16 PC, 8 slsts, 4 x 8ch-sp)

Fasten off colour 4.

Round 16: Join colour 5 to 8ch-sp, *10 hdc in 8ch-sp, 3 dc in first PC, 2 tr in next PC, 2 ch, 2 tr in next PC (corner), 3 dc in last PC; rep from * to end. (40 hdc, 24 dc, 16 tr, 4 x 2ch-sp corners)

Fasten off colour 5.

Round 17: Join colour 6 in 2ch-sp, *(3 dc, 1 ch, 3 dc) in 2ch-sp, 8 dc, dc2tog twice, 8 dc; rep from * to end. (96 dc, 4 x 1ch-sp corners)

Fasten off and weave in ends.

BLOOMING PINWHEEL

DESIGNER: ANA MORAIS SOARES

YARN

Rosários4 Regata, light worsted (DK), in foll shades:
Colour 1: Yellow (31)
Colour 2: Green (26)
Colour 3: Light Blush Pink (23)
Colour 4: Blush Pink (21)
Colour 5: White Pearl (01)

HOOK

US size E/4 (3.5mm) hook

GAUGE (TENSION)

A single motif measures approx 7in (18cm) using a US size E/4 (3.5mm) hook.

SPECIAL ABBREVIATIONS

V-st, (1 dc, 2 ch, 1 dc) in same st
4dc-cl, cluster of 4 dc

PATTERN

Using E/4 hook and colour 1, make a magic ring.

Round 1: 1 ch (does not count as st throughout), 6 sc in ring, slst in first sc to join. Do not close ring. (6 sc)

Round 2: 1 ch, 12 hdc in ring, working over sc from Round 1, sl st in first hdc to join. Close ring. (12 hdc)

Round 3: 1 ch, 1 scFLO in each st around, slst in first sc to join or make invisible join. (12 sc)

Fasten off colour 1.

Round 4: Join colour 2, working in Round 2 sts, [1 scBLO, 2 scBLO in next st] around, slst in first sc to join. (18 sc)

Round 5: 5 ch (counts as 1 dc, 2 ch), 1 dc in same st (first V-st made), *skip one st, V-st in next st; rep from * to end, slst in 3rd ch of beg 5-ch to join. (9 V-sts)

Fasten off colour 2.

Round 6: Join colour 3, [1 sc in sp between 2 V-sts, 3 ch, 4dc-cl in next 2ch-sp, 3 ch] 9 times, slst in first sc to join. (9 sc, 9 clusters, 18 x 3ch-sp)

Fasten off colour 3.

Round 7: Join colour 4, [1 FPsc around 4dc-cl, slst in next 3ch-sp, 3 ch (counts as 1 dc), 5 dc in same 3ch-sp, skip sc, sl st in next 3ch-sp] 9 times, slst in first FPsc to join. (9 FPsc, 54 dc, 18 slsts)

Fasten off colour 4. Turn work.

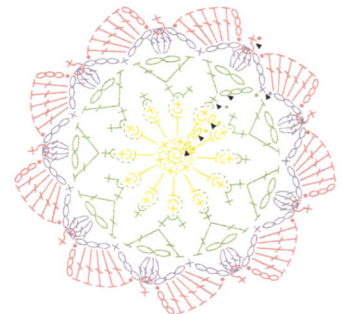

ROUNDS 1-7

Round 8 (WS): Join colour 5, [1 slst catching back legs of sc from Round 6, 5 ch] 9 times, slst in first slst to join. Turn work. (9 slsts, 9 x 5ch-sp)

Round 9 (RS): Sl st in 5ch-sp, 3 ch (counts as 1 dc throughout), 5 dc in same 5ch-sp, *[5 dc in next 5ch-sp] twice, 6 dc in next 5ch-sp; rep from * twice more omitting last 6-dc group, slst in top of beg 3-ch to join. (48 dc)

Round 10: 3 ch, (1 dc, 2 ch, 2 dc) in same st (first corner made), *1 dc, 9 hdc, 1 dc, (2 dc, 2 ch, 2 dc) in next st (corner made); rep from * 3 more times omitting last corner sts, slst in top of beg 3-ch to join. (24 dc, 36 hdc, 4 x 2ch-sp corners)

Round 11: 2 ch (counts as 1 hdc), hdcBLO in next st, *(2 hdc, 2 ch, 2 hdc) in next 2ch-sp corner, 15 hdcBLO; rep from * 3 more times omitting last 2 hdcBLO, slst in top of beg 2-ch to join. (76 hdc, 4 x 2ch-sp corners)

Fasten off colour 5.

Round 12: Join colour 2, *1 dc in 2ch-sp corner, 1 tr in 2ch-sp corner of Round 10 in middle of 4-hdc worked there, working in front of current 2ch-sp, (1 dc, 2 ch, 1 dc) in 2ch-sp of current round (corner made), 1 tr in 2ch-sp corner of Round 10 in middle of 4-hdc worked there, working in front of current 2ch-sp, 1 dc in current 2ch-sp, skip first st (is a bit hidden), 1 dc in next st, 1 trFLO in first st from Round 10, skip next st (behind trFLO), 6 dc, 2 trFLO in corresponding sts of Round 10, skip next 2 sts (behind 2 trFLO), 6 dc, 1 trFLO in last st of Round 10, skip next st (behind trFLO), 1 dc in last st before 2ch-sp corner; rep from * 3 more times, slst in first dc to join. (24 tr, 76 dc, 4 x 2ch-sp corners)

Fasten off colour 2.

Round 13: Join colour 5, *(1 sc, 2 ch, 1 sc) in 2ch-sp corner, 1 scBLO, 1 FPhdc, 2 scBLO, 1 FPhdc, 6 scBLO, 2 FPhdc, 6 scBLO, 1 FPhdc, 2 scBLO, 1 FPhdc, 1 scBLO; rep from * 3 more times, slst in beg sc to join. (24 FPhdc, 80 sc, 4 x 2ch-sp corner)

Fasten off colour 5.

Round 14: Join colour 4, *(1 hdc, 2 ch, 1 hdc) in 2ch-sp corner, 26 hdcBLO; rep from * 3 more times, slst in first hdc to join. (112 hdc, 4 x 2ch-sp corners)

Fasten off colour 4.

Round 15: Join colour 3 working entire round in 3rd loop of hdc from prev round (loop behind "v" of st), *(2 hdc, 2 ch, 2 hdc) in 2ch-sp corner, 28 hdc; rep from * 3 more times, slst in first hdc to join. (128 hdc, 4 x 2ch-sp corners)

Fasten off colour 3.

Round 16: Join colour 1, *(2 dc, 2 ch, 2 dc) in 2ch-sp corner, [skip next 2 sts, V-st in next st] 10 times, skip last 2 sts; rep from * 3 more times, slst in first dc to join. (40 V-sts, 16 dc, 4 x 2ch-sp corners)

Fasten off colour 1.

Round 17: Join colour 3, *(2 hdc, 2 ch, 2 hdc) in 2ch-sp corner, skip first st, 1 hdc in next st, 1 hdc in space between 2nd corner dc and first V-st from previous round, 2 hdc in 2ch-sp of next V-st, [1 hdc in next sp between V-sts, 2 hdc in 2 ch-sp of next V-st] 9 times, 1 hdc in sp between last V-st and first corner dc from previous round, 2 hdc; rep from * 3 more times, slst in first hdc to join. (152 hdc, 4 x 2ch-sp corners)

Fasten off colour 3.

Round 18: Join colour 4 in corner, *(1 sc, 2 ch, 1 sc) in same sp, skip first st, [1 scBLO, 1 sc in both loops of next st] 18 times, 1 scBLO in next st; rep from * 3 more times, slst in first sc to join. (156 sc, 4 x 2ch-sp corners)

Round 19: 1 ch (does not count as st), sc in same st, *(1 sc, 1 hdc, 1 sc) in 2ch-sp corner, 39 sc; rep from * 3 more times, omitting last sc, slst in first sc to join. (164 sc, 4 hdc corner sts)

Fasten off and weave in ends.

ROUNDS 8-19

FLORAL BURST

DESIGNER: CATHERINE NORONHA

YARN

Stylecraft Special DK, light worsted (DK), in foll shades:
Colour 1: Mustard (1823)
Colour 2: Teal (1062)
Colour 3: Petrol (1708)
Colour 4: Boysenberry (1828)
Colour 5: Cream (1005)

HOOK

US size E/4 (3.5mm) hook

GAUGE (TENSION)

A single motif measures approx 7½in (19cm) from top to bottom using a US size E/4 (3.5mm) hook.

SPECIAL ABBREVIATION

2dc-cl, cluster of 2 dc

NOTES

Motif is worked in tapestry crochet from Round 3 onward.
Change to next colour on last yoh of prev st. Carry unused yarn and crochet over. Make joining slst at end of each round around unused yarn to carry it up for next round.

From Round 2 onward, each round starts with 3 ch, which counts as 1 dc, 1 ch. This is final dc of one side of motif, plus ch to form first corner ch-sp. Other corner ch-sps are formed of 2 ch.

PATTERN

Change colour foll chart.

Using E/4 hook and colour 1, make a magic ring.

Round 1 (RS): Working into ring, 2 ch, 1 dc (counts as 2dc-cl), 1 ch, [2dc-cl, 2 ch] 5 times, slst in beg dc to join. (6 x 2dc-cl, 1 x 1ch-sp corner, 5 x 2ch-sp corners)

Fasten off colour 1.

Round 2: Join colour 2 to any ch-sp, 3 ch (counts as 1 dc, 1 ch throughout), 1 dc in ch-sp, *1 dc, (1 dc, 2 ch, 1 dc) in 2ch-sp; rep from * 4 more times, 1 dc, slst in 2nd ch of beg 3-ch, slst in ch-sp to join. (18 dc, 1 x 1ch-sp corner, 5 x 2ch-sp corners)

Round 3: 3 ch, 1 dc in ch-sp, *3 dc, (1 dc, 2 ch, 1 dc) in 2ch-sp; rep from * 4 more times, 3 dc, slst in 2nd ch of beg 3-ch, slst in ch-sp to join. (30 dc, 1 x 1ch-sp corner, 5 x 2ch-sp corners)

Round 4: 3 ch, 1 dc in ch-sp, *5 dc, (1 dc, 2 ch, 1 dc) in 2ch-sp; rep from * 4 more times; 5 dc, slst in 2nd ch of beg 3-ch, slst in ch-sp to join. (42 dc, 1 x 1ch-sp corner, 5 x 2ch-sp corners)

Round 5: 3 ch, 1 dc in ch-sp, *7 dc, (1 dc, 2 ch, 1 dc) in 2ch-sp; rep from * 4 more times, 7 dc, slst in 2nd ch of beg 3-ch, slst in ch-sp to join. (54 dc, 1 x 1ch-sp corner, 5 x 2ch-sp corners)

Round 6: 3 ch, 1 dc in ch-sp, *9 dc, (1 dc, 2 ch, 1 dc) in 2ch-sp; rep from * 4 more times, 9 dc, slst in 2nd ch of beg 3-ch, slst in ch-sp to join. (66 dc, 1 x 1ch-sp corner, 5 x 2ch-sp corners)

Round 7: 3 ch, 1 dc in ch-sp, *11 dc, (1 dc, 2 ch, 1 dc) in 2ch-sp; rep from * 4 more times; 11 dc, slst in 2nd ch of beg 3-ch, slst in ch-sp to join. (78 dc, 1 x 1ch-sp corner, 5 x 2ch-sp corners)

Round 8: 1 ch (does not count as st), (1 sc, 2 dc, 1 sc) in ch-sp, *13 sc, (1 sc, 2 dc, 1 sc) in 2ch-sp; rep from * 4 more times, 13 sc, slst in beg sc to join. (90 sc, 1 x 1ch-sp corner, 5 x 2ch-sp corners)

Fasten off and weave in ends.

Chart illustrates one side of hexagon; it should be repeated six times on each round.

Each square represents one dc stitch, except in Round 1, where square represents one 2dc-cl, and in Round 8, where each square represents one sc stitch.

Read all chart rows from right to left.

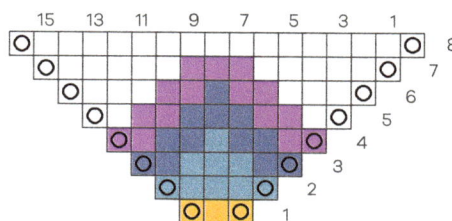

KEY

🟧	Colour 1
🟦	Colour 2
🟦	Colour 3
🟪	Colour 4
⬜	Colour 5
O	chain (ch)

CIRCE

DESIGNER: HATTIE RISDALE

YARN

Phildar Phil Coton 4, light worsted (DK), in foll shades:
Colour 1: Cyan (1362)
Colour 2: Craie (1937)
Colour 3: Rosee (1149)

HOOK

US size G/6 (4mm) hook

GAUGE (TENSION)

A single motif measures approx 6¾in (17cm) using a US size G/6 (4mm) hook.

SPECIAL ABBREVIATION

5tr-cl, cluster of 5 tr

PATTERN

Using G/6 hook and colour 1, make a magic ring.

Round 1: Working in ring, 4 ch (counts as 1 dc, 1 ch), *1 dc, 1 ch; rep from * 11 more times, slst in 3rd ch of beg 4-ch to join, do not fasten off. (12 dc, 12 ch)

Round 2: Slst in 1ch-sp, 1 ch (counts as 1 sc), 1 sc in same sp, 2 sc in each sp around, slst in beg 1-ch to join, do not fasten off. (24 sc)

Round 3: 3 ch (counts as first part of 5tr-cl) complete 5tr-cl in same sp, 3 ch, *skip 1 st, (5tr-cl, 3 ch) in next st; rep from * around, slst in top of beg 5tr-cl to join, do not fasten off. (12 x 5tr-cl, 12 x 3ch-sp)

Round 4: 1 ch (counts as 1 sc), *1 sc in first ch of 3-ch, 3 sc in ch-sp, 1 sc in top of 5tr-cl, rep from * around omitting sc in top of 5tr-cl on last rep, slst in beg 1-ch to join. (60 sc)

Fasten off colour 1.

Round 5: Join colour 2 with slst in top of any sc in first ch of 3-ch, 3 ch (counts as first part of 5tr-cl), complete 5tr-cl, 2 ch, (1 dc, 2 ch) in 3rd sc of 3 sc, *(5tr-cl, 2 ch) in first ch of 3-ch, (1 dc, 2 ch) in 3rd sc of 3 sc; rep from * around, slst in top of beg 5tr-cl to join, do not fasten off. (12 x 5tr-cl, 12 dc, 24 x 2ch-sp)

Round 6: 2 ch (counts as 1 hdc), *4 hdc in 2ch-sp after 5tr-cl, 3 hdc in next 2ch-sp, 1 hdc in top of 5tr-cl; rep from * around omitting hdc in top of 5tr-cl on last rep, slst in 2nd of beg 2-ch to join. (96 hdc)

Fasten off colour 2.

Round 7: Join colour 3 with slst in any sp between two sets of hdc (above 1-dc in Round 5), 3 ch (counts as first part of 5tr-cl), (complete 5tr-cl, 2 ch, 5tr-cl) in same sp, (2 ch, 1 hdc) in sp between two hdc groups (above 5tr-cl), [(2 ch, 1 hdc) in sp between next two hdc groups] twice, 2 ch, *(5tr-cl, 2 ch, 5tr-cl) in sp between next two hdc groups, [(2 ch, 1 hdc) in sp between two hdc groups] 3 times, 2 ch; rep from * around, slst in top of beg 5tr-cl to join, do not fasten off. (12 x 5tr-cl, 18 hdc, 30 x 2ch-sp)

Round 8: 2 ch (counts as 1 hdc), *(2 hdc, 2 ch, 2 hdc) in corner 2ch-sp, 3 hdc in next 2ch-sp, 4 hdc in next two 2ch-sp, 3 hdc in next 2ch-sp; rep from * around omitting final hdc on last rep, slst in top of beg 2-ch to join. (108 hdc, 6 x 2ch-sp)

Fasten off and weave in all ends.

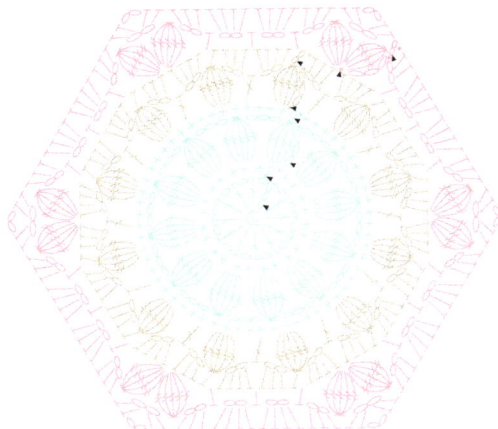

DAISY GIRL

DESIGNER: JULIE YEAGER

YARN

Scheepjes Stone Washed, sport (4ply), in foll shades:
Colour 1: Blue Apatite (805)
Colour 2: Beryl (833)
Colour 3: Moon Stone (801)

HOOK

US size G/6 (4mm) hook

GAUGE (TENSION)

A single motif measures approx 8in (20cm) using a US size G/6 (4mm) hook.

SPECIAL ABBREVIATIONS

spike sc, sc worked in st two or more rows below
V-st, (1 dc, 3 ch, 1 dc) in same st

NOTE

In Round 8 space between 5-sc groups is not a ch sp.

PATTERN

Using G/6 hook and colour 1, 5 ch, slst to join into a ring.

Round 1: 3 ch (counts as 1 dc throughout), 15 dc in ring, slst in top of beg 3-ch to join. (16 dc)

Fasten off colour 1.

Round 2: Join colour 2 with slst in any st, 6 ch (counts as 1 dc, 3 ch), 1 dc in same st, [skip 1 st, V-st in next st] 7 times, skip 1 st, slst in 3rd ch of beg 6-ch to join. (8 V-sts)

Fasten off colour 2.

Round 3: Join colour 1 with slst in any 3ch-sp, 2 ch (counts as 1 hdc throughout), 3 hdc in same sp, [4 hdc in next 3ch-sp] 7 times, slst in top of beg 2-ch to join. (32 hdc)

Fasten off colour 1.

Round 4: Join colour 3 with slst in any st, 5 ch (counts as 1 dc, 2 ch), [skip 1 st, (1 dc, 2 ch) in next st] 15 times, slst in 3rd ch of beg 5-ch to join. (16 dc, 16 ch-2 sp)

Fasten off colour 3.

Round 5: Join colour 1 with slst in any skipped hdc from Round 3, 3 ch, working around and enclosing 2ch-sp, 2 dc in same st, [working around and enclosing 2ch-sp, 3 dc in next skipped st from Round 3] 15 times, slst in top of beg 3-ch to join. (48 dc)

Fasten off colour 1.

Round 6: Join colour 2 with sc in 3rd dc of any 3-dc group, 2 sc, [2 ch, 3 sc] 15 times, 2 ch, slst in first sc to join. (48 sc, 16 ch-2 sp)

Fasten off colour 2.

Round 7: Join colour 1 with sc in any ch-2 sp, 4 sc in same sp, [5 sc in next ch-2 sp] 15 times, slst in first st to join. (80 sc)

Fasten off colour 1.

Round 8: Work each st in space between 5-sc groups. Join colour 3 with sc in any space between 5-sc groups, [1 ch, 7 dc in space between next group, 1 ch, 1 sc in space between next group] 7 times, 1 ch, 7 dc in space between next group, 1 ch, slst in first sc to join. (56 dc, 8 sc, 16 ch)

Fasten off colour 3.

Round 9: Join colour 1 with sc in first dc of any group, 6 sc, [spike sc in 4th sc of 5-sc group from Round 7, skip (1 ch, 1 sc, 1 ch) of Round 8, spike sc in 2nd sc of 5-sc group from Round 7, 7 sc] 7 times, spike sc in 4th sc of 5-sc group from Round 7, skip (1 ch, 1 sc, 1 ch) of Round 8, spike sc in 2nd sc of 5-sc group from Round 7, slst in first st to join. (72 sc)

Fasten off colour 1.

Round 10: Join colour 2 with slstBLO in first sc after any spike sc, 3 ch, 1 dcBLO in same st, *1 hdcBLO, 4 scBLO, 2 scBLO in next st, dc2togBLO, 2 scBLO in next st, 4 scBLO, 1 hdcBLO, 2 dcBLO in next st, [2 trBLO in next st] twice, 2 dcBLO in next st; rep from * twice more, 1 hdcBLO, 4 scBLO, 2 scBLO in next st, dc2togBLO, 2 scBLO in next st, 4 scBLO, 1 hdcBLO, 2 dcBLO in next st, [2 trBLO in next st] twice, slst in top of beg 3-ch to join. (92 sts)

Round 11: 3 ch, 1 dc, [1 hdc, 14 sc, 1 hdc, 3 dc, (2 dc, 1 ch, 2 dc) in next st for corner, 3 dc] 3 times, 1 hdc, 14 sc, 1 hdc, 3 dc, (2 dc, 1 ch, 2 dc) in next st, 1 dc, slst in top of beg 3-ch to join. (104 sts, 4 x 1ch-sp corners)

Fasten off colour 2.

Round 12: Join colour 1 with sc in any ch-1 sp, 2 ch, 1 sc in same sp, [1 sc, 1 FPdc, 22 sc, 1 FPdc, 1 sc, (1 sc, 2 ch, 1 sc) in 1ch-sp] 3 times, 1 sc, 1 FPdc, 22 sc, 1 FPdc, 1 sc, slst in first sc to join. (112 sts, 4 x 2ch-sp corners)

Fasten off and weave in ends.

COUNTRY POSY

DESIGNER: CAITIE MOORE

YARN

Nurturing Fibres Eco-Cotton, light worsted (DK), in foll shades:
Colour 1: Sunglow
Colour 2: Aventurine
Colour 3: Vanilla
Colour 4: Persian
Colour 5: Lime
Colour 6: Watershed

HOOK

US size G/6 (4mm) hook.

GAUGE (TENSION)

A single motif measures approx 6in (15cm) using a US size G/6 (4mm) hook.

SPECIAL ABBREVIATIONS

3dc-PC, popcorn of 3 dc, 1 ch
modPC1, 3 dc in first st, 2ch-picot, 3 dc in next st, pull up loop, remove hook, insert hook from front to back through first dc, catch working loop and pull through, 1 ch
modPC2, 2 dc, 2ch-picot, 2 dc, in same st, pull up loop, remove hook, insert hook from front to back through first dc of st, catch loop and pull through, 1 ch
2ch-picot, picot with 2 ch
3ch-picot, picot with 3 ch

NOTES

Join yarn with standing sts unless otherwise indicated, and join round with invisible join in standing st.
In Round 10 space between PCs is a gap not a ch sp.

PATTERN

Using G/6 hook and colour 1, make a magic ring.

Round 1: 8 sc in ring, pull on tail to close ring. (8 sc)

Fasten off colour 1.

Round 2: Join colour 2 in any st, *(1 scFLO, 1 hdcFLO, 1 scFLO in same st; rep from * to end. (24 sts)

Fasten off colour 2.

Round 3: Join colour 3 in BLO from Round 1, 2 hdcBLO in each st. (16 hdc)

Fasten off colour 3.

Round 4: Join colour 3 in any st, *(1 dc, 1 ch, 1 dc) in same st, 4 ch, skip 3 sts; rep from * to end. (8 dc, 4 ch, 4 x 4ch-sp)

Fasten off colour 3.

Round 5: Join colour 1 to Round 3 in first hdc after dc, *with 4ch-sp in back, work three 3dc-PC, 2 ch (skip over dcs from Round 4), skip 1 hdc; rep from * to end. (12 PC, 4 x 2ch-sp)

Fasten off colour 1.

continued on next page >

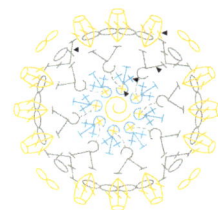

ROUNDS 1-5

Round 6: Join colour 4 in 4ch-sp from Round 4, *10 dc in 4ch-sp, skip dc, 2 dc in 1ch-sp, skip dc; rep from * to end. (48 dc)

Fasten off colour 4.

Round 7: Join colour 3 in first dc of 10-dc group, *10 scBLO, keep 2-ch from Round 5 to back, 1 FPdc around dc from Round 4, 2 scBLO, 1 FPdc around next dc from Round 4; rep from * to end. (56 sts)

Fasten off colour 3.

Round 8: Join colour 5 in the first FPdc (of a pair) from prev round, *1 sc, modPC1, 1 sc in next FPdc, 8 ch; rep from * to end. (4 modPC1, 8 sc, 4 x 8ch-sp)

Fasten off colour 5.

Round 9: Join colour 3 to Round 7 FPdc to right of any modPC1, *1 FPdc around FPdc from Round 7, now work in Round 8 around modPC1, (1 sc, 3dc-PC) in sc from Round 8, 3 3dc-PC in 1ch-sp at top of modPC1, (3dc-PC, 1 sc) in sc, 1 FPdc around next FPdc from Round 7, 10 sc in Round 7; rep from * to end, keeping ch from prev round in back. (20 PC, 48 sc, 8 dc)

Fasten off colour 3.

Round 10: Join colour 6 to sc to left of rightmost FPdc, between FPdc and PC, *2 hdc in same st, skip PC, [2 hdc in space between PC, skip PC] twice, (1 hdc, 2-ch picot, 1 hdc) in space between PC, [skip PC, 2 hdc in space between PC] twice, 2 hdc in sc, skip FPdc, sc2tog, skip 6 sts from Round 9 and work in FLO from Round 6, 6 dcFLO, work back in Round 9, sc2tog, skip FPdc; rep from * to end. (88 sts, 4 picot)

Fasten off colour 6.

Round 11: Join colour 3 to first hdc at base of a petal (bottom right), *1 hdc in 3rd loop of next 6 hdc, 2 hdc in 3rd loop of same st, skip picot, 3ch-picot, 2 hdc in 3rd loop of same st, 1 hdc in 3rd loop of next 6 hdc, 3 scBLO, sc2togBLO, 3 scBLO; rep from * to end. (92 sts)

Fasten off colour 3.

Round 12: Join colour 2 in any sc2tog, *(1 sc, modPC2, 1 sc) in same st, 12 ch (keeping ch in back); rep from * to end. (4 modPC2, 8 sc, 4 x 12ch-sp)

Fasten off colour 2.

Round 13: Join colour 3 in rightmost hdc at base of a petal in Round 11, *7 dcBLO, 2 dcBLO in same st, 3ch-picot, 2 dcBLO in same st, 10 dcBLO, 1 ch behind PC, 3 dcBLO; rep from * to end. (96 dc, 4 ch, 4 picot)

Fasten off colour 3.

Round 14: Join colour 4 in 1 ch-sp, *2 hdc in 1ch-sp, skip 1 st, 11 scBLO, 3 ch, skip picot, 11 scBLO, skip 1 st; rep from * to end. (96 sts, 4 x 3ch-sp corners)

Fasten off and weave in ends.

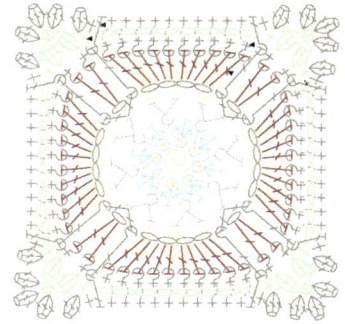

ROUNDS 6-9

ROUNDS 10-11

ROUNDS 12-14

MARINE FLOWER

DESIGNER: ANNA NIKIPIROWICZ

YARN

Rowan Felted Tweed, light worsted (DK), in foll shades:

Colour 1: Fjord (218)
Colour 2: Duck Egg (173)
Colour 3: Clay (177)

HOOK

US size E/4 (3.5mm) hook

GAUGE (TENSION)

A single motif measures approx 7in (18cm) from point to point using a US size E/4 (3.5mm) hook.

SPECIAL ABBREVIATION

V-st, (1 dc, 2 ch, 1 dc) in same st

NOTE

Join yarn with standing sts unless otherwise indicated, and join round with invisible join in standing st.

PATTERN

Using E/4 hook and colour 1, make a magic ring.

Round 1: 1 ch (does not count as st), 8 hdc in ring, enclosing yarn end as you work, pull on yarn end to close opening, slst in first hdc to join. (8 hdc)

Round 2: 1 ch, 1 hdc, 1 ch, [1 hdc, 1 ch] 7 times, make invisible join in beg hdc. (8 hdc, 8 ch-sp)

Fasten off colour 1.

Round 3: Join colour 2, 1 stsc in first hdc, (1 hdc, 1 dc, 2 ch, 1 dc, 1 hdc) in 1ch-sp, *1 sc, (1 hdc, 1 dc, 2 ch, 1 dc, 1 hdc) in 1ch-sp, *rep from * to end. (16 hdc, 16 dc, 8 sc, 8 x 2ch-sp)

Fasten off colour 2.

Round 4: Join colour 3, 1 stdc in first sc, 2 ch, 1 dc in same st, skip next 2 sts, 1 sc in next 2ch-sp, skip next 2 sts, *V-st in next st, skip next 2 sts, 1 sc in next 2ch-sp, skip next 2 sts; rep from * to end. (8 V-sts, 8 sc)

Fasten off colour 3.

Round 5: Join colour 1, 1 sthdc in first 2ch-sp, (2 dc, 2 ch, 2 dc, 1 hdc) in same ch-sp, skip next st, 1 sc in sc, skip next st, *(1 hdc, 2 dc, 2 ch, 2 dc, 1 hdc) in next 2ch-sp, skip next st, 1 sc, skip next st; rep from * to end. (32 dc, 16 hdc, 8 sc, 8 x 2ch-sp)

Fasten off colour 1.

Round 6: Join colour 3, 1 sttr in first sc, 5 ch, 1 tr in same st, skip next 3 sts, 1 sc in 2ch-sp, skip next 3 sts, *(1 tr, 5 ch, 1 tr) in next st, skip next 3 sts, 1 sc in 2ch-sp, skip next 3 sts; rep from * to end. (16 tr, 8 x 5ch-sp)

Fasten off colour 3.

Round 7: Join colour 2, 1 sthdc in first 5ch-sp, (1 hdc, 2 dc, 1 tr, 2 ch, 1 tr, 2 dc, 2 hdc) in same ch-sp, skip next st, 1 sc in sc, skip next st, *(2 hdc, 2 dc, 1 tr, 2 ch, 1 tr, 2 dc, 2 hdc) in 5ch-sp, skip next st, 1 sc in next sc, skip next st; rep from * to end. (32 hdc, 32 dc, 16 tr, 8 sc, 8 x 2ch-sp)

Fasten off colour 2.

Round 8: Join colour 3, 1 stsc in first 2ch-sp, 2 ch, 1 sc in same sp, 3 ch, skip 2 sts, dc2tog working one leg in next st, skip 5 sts, work 2nd leg in 6th st, 3 ch, skip next 2 sts, *(1 sc, 2 ch, 1 sc) in 2ch-sp, 3 ch, skip 2 sts, dc2tog working one leg in next st, skip next 5 sts, work 2nd leg in 6th st, 3 ch, skip next 2 sts; rep from * to end. (16 x 3ch-sp, 16 sc, 8 dc, 8 x 2ch-sp corners)

Fasten off colour 3.

Round 9: Join colour 1, 1 stsc in first 2ch-sp, 2 ch, 1 sc in same sp, 1 sc, 5 sc in next 3ch-sp, 1 sc, 5 sc in next 3ch-sp, *1 sc, (1 sc, 2 ch, 1 sc) in next 2ch-sp, 1 sc, 5 sc in next 3ch-sp, 1 sc, 5 sc in next 3ch-sp; rep from * to last st, 1 sc. (120 sc, 8 x 2ch-sp corners)

Fasten off colour 1.

Round 10: Join colour 2, 1 stsc in first 2ch-sp, 2 ch, 1 sc in same sp, 6 sc, sc3tog, 6 sc, *(1 sc, 2 ch, 1 sc) in next 2ch-sp, 6 sc, sc3tog, 6 sc; rep from * to end. (120 sc, 8 x 2ch-sp corners)

Fasten off with invisible join, weave in all ends.

LOTUS BLOSSOM

DESIGNER: CAITIE MOORE

YARN

Nurturing Fibres Eco-Cotton, light worsted (DK), in foll shades:
Colour 1: Persian
Colour 2: Aventurine
Colour 3: Sunglow
Colour 4: Charcoal
Colour 5: Vanilla

HOOK

US size G/6 (4mm) hook

GAUGE (TENSION)

A single motif measures approx 6¼in (16cm) using a US size G/6 (4mm) hook.

SPECIAL ABBREVIATIONS

4dc-bobble, bobble of 4 dc
FP-bobble, 4dc-bobble worked round front post of st
2ch-picot, picot with 2 ch
3ch-picot, picot with 3 ch

NOTE

Join yarn with standing sts unless otherwise indicated, and join round with invisible join in standing st.

PATTERN

Using G/6 hook and colour 1, make a magic ring.

Round 1: 1 ch (does not count as st), 8 sc in ring. (8 sc)

Fasten off colour 1.

Round 2: Join colour 2 in any st, 2 sc in each st to end. (16 sc)

Fasten off colour 2.

Round 3: Join colour 3 in any st, *1 sc, 4dc-bobble; rep from * to end. (8 bobbles, 8 sc)

Fasten off colour 3.

Round 4: Join colour 4 in any sc, *3 sc in same st, 1 ch, skip bobble; rep from * to end. (24 sc, 8 ch)

Fasten off colour 4.

Round 5: Join colour 5 in any 1ch-sp, *(1 slst, 1 ch, 3 dc, 2ch-picot, 2 dc, 1 ch, 1 slst) in 1ch-sp, 1 ch, skip 3 sc; rep from * to end. (8 petals, 8 ch, 16 slst)

Fasten off colour 5.

Round 6: Join colour 2 in any 1ch-sp between petals from prev round, *1 sc, skip slst, skip 1 ch, 5 BPdc, skip 1 ch, skip slst; rep from * to end. (40 dc, 8 sc)

Fasten off colour 2.

Round 7: Join colour 2 in any sc, *1 slst, 1 sc, 1 hdc, (2 dc, 3ch-picot, 2 dc) in same st, 1 hdc, 1 sc; rep from * to end. (72 sts, 8 picot)

Fasten off colour 2.

Round 8 (WS): Join colour 2 around post of 3rd dc from any 5-BPdc group from Round 6, *1 FPsc, 3 ch, 1 FPsc around 3rd BPdc of next petal, 3 ch; rep from * to end. (8 sc, 8 x 3ch-sp)

Fasten off colour 2.

Round 9 (RS): Join colour 5 in any 3 ch-sp, *(4 sc, 3 ch, 1 sc in 2nd ch from hook, 1 hdc in 3rd ch from hook, 4 sc) in 3ch-sp; rep from * in each 3ch-sp. (104 sts)

Fasten off colour 5.

Round 10: Join colour 4 in 2nd sc to left of any Round 9 petal, *1 hdc, 1 dc, 2 dc in next st, 2 ch, 2 dc in next st, 1 dc, 1 hdc, 1 ch (work behind Round 9 petal), skip sc, skip petal, skip sc, 6 hdc, 1 ch, skip sc, skip petal, skip sc; rep from * to end. (64 sts, 4 x 2ch-sp corners)

Fasten off colour 4.

Round 11: Join colour 4 in any 2ch-sp, *(2 dc, 2 ch, 2 dc) in 2ch-sp, skip next st, 3 dc, 1 dc in 1ch-sp, skip next st, 5 dc, 1 dc in 1ch-

ROUNDS 1-7

ROUNDS 8-14

sp, 3 dc; rep from * to end. (68 dc, 4 x 2ch-sp corners)

Fasten off colour 4.

Round 12: Join colour 1 in any 2ch-sp, (1 hdc, 2 dc, 1 ch, 2 dc, 1 hdc) in 2ch-sp, skip next st, 7 scBLO, 1 sc, FP-bobble in same st, 1 sc, 7 scBLO; rep from * to end. (88 sts, 4 bobbles, 4 x 1ch-sp corners)

Fasten off colour 1.

Round 13: Join colour 3 in any 1ch-sp, *(2 hdc, 1 ch, 2 hdc) in 1ch-sp, skip 1 st, 10 hdc, skip bobble, 10 hdc, skip 1 st; rep from * to end. (96 hdc, 4 x 1ch-sp corners)

Fasten off colour 3.

Round 14: Join colour 4 in any 1ch-sp, *(2 hdc, 1 ch, 2 hdc) in 1ch-sp, skip 1 st, [2 hdc in next st, skip 1 st] 11 times, 2 hdc in next st; rep from * to end. (112 hdc, 4 x 1ch-sp corners)

Fasten off and weave in ends.

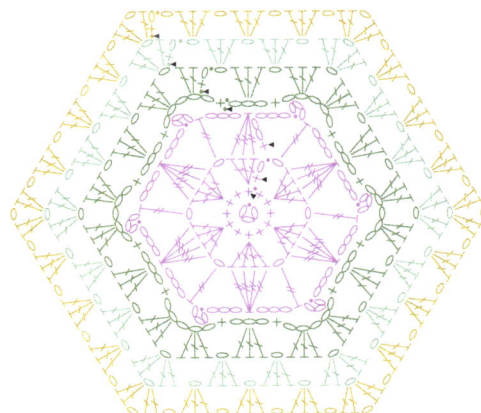

FLORAL HEXAGON

DESIGNER: RACHELE CARMONA

YARN

Scheepjes Stone Washed, sport (4ply), in foll shades:
Colour 1: Garnet (810)
Colour 2: Canada Jade (806)
Colour 3: New Jade (819)
Colour 4: Yellow Jasper (809)

HOOK

US size G/6 (4mm) hook

GAUGE (TENSION)

A single motif measures approx 6in (15cm) from top to bottom using a US size G/6 (4mm) hook.

SPECIAL ABBREVIATION

3ch-picot, picot with 3 ch

PATTERN

Using G/6 hook and colour 1, 3 ch, slst to join into a ring.

Round 1: 12 sc in ring, slst in first sc to join. (12 sc)

Round 2: (1 sc, 1 ch) in next st (counts as first dc throughout), 3 dc in same st, [1 ch, skip 1 st, 4 dc in next st] 5 times, 1 ch, slst in first dc to join. (24 dc, 6 x 1ch-sp corners)

Round 3: (1 sc, 2 ch) in same st as slst (counts as first tr), tr3tog, [3 ch, tr in ch-sp, 3ch-picot, 3 ch, tr4tog] 5 times, 3 ch, tr in ch-sp, 3ch-picot, 3 ch, slst in tr3tog. (6 x tr4tog, 6 picot, 6 tr, 12 x 3ch-sp)

Fasten off colour 1.

Round 4: Join colour 2 with slst in first 3ch-sp of Round 3, 1 sc in same sp, [5 ch, 1 sc in next ch-sp, 3 ch, 1 sc in next ch-sp] 6 times omitting final sc, slst in first sc to join. (12 sc, 6 x 5ch-sp, 6 x 3ch-sp)

Round 5: (1 sc, 1 ch) in first ch-sp, (2 dc, 1 ch, 3 dc) in same sp, *1 ch, 3 dc in next ch-sp, 1 ch, (3 dc, 1 ch, 3 dc) in next ch-sp, rep from * 4 times, 1 ch, 3dc in next ch-sp, 1 ch, slst in first dc to join. (54 dc, 18 ch-sp)

Fasten off colour 2.

Round 6: Join colour 3 with slst in first 1ch-sp, (1 sc, 1 ch, 1 dc, 1 ch, 2 dc) all in same sp, *[1 ch, 3 dc in next ch-sp] twice, 1 ch, (2 dc, 1 ch, 2 dc) in next ch-sp, rep from * 4 times, [1 ch, 3 dc in next ch-sp] twice, 1 ch, slst in first dc to join. (60 dc, 24 ch-sp)

Fasten off colour 3.

Round 7: Join colour 4 with slst in first ch-1 sp, (1 sc, 1 ch, 1 dc, 1 ch, 2dc) all in same sp, *[1 ch, 3 dc in next ch-sp] 3 times, 1 ch, (2 dc, 1 ch, 2 dc) in next ch-sp, rep from * 4 times, [1 ch, 3 dc in next ch-sp] 3 times, 1 ch, slst in first dc to join. (78 dc, 30 ch-sp)

Fasten off and weave in ends.

GROW YOUR GARDEN

DESIGNER: ANA MORAIS SOARES

. . . .

YARN

Rosários4 Abraço, light worsted (DK), in foll shades:

Colour 1: White Pearl (01)
Colour 2: Pink (23)
Colour 3: Yellow (13)

HOOK

US size E/4 (3.5mm) hook

GAUGE (TENSION)

A single motif measures approx 7½in (19cm) using a US size E/4 (3.5mm) hook.

SPECIAL ABBREVIATIONS

V-st, (1 dc, 2 ch, 1 dc) in same st
2dc-cl, cluster of 2 dc
3dc-cl, cluster of 3 dc
4dc-bobble, bobble of 4 dc
2tr-cl, cluster of 2 tr

PATTERN

Using E/4 hook and colour 1, make a magic ring.

Round 1: 3 ch (counts as first dc of 3dc-cl), complete 3dc-cl, 3 ch, [3dc-cl, 3 ch] 5 times in ring, slst in top of 3-ch to join. (6 clusters, 6 x 3ch-sp)

Fasten off colour 1.

Round 2: Join colour 2,3 ch (counts as first dc of 3dc-cl), complete 3dc-cl, 3 ch, [3dc-cl in 3ch-sp, 1 FPdc around next st, 3dc-cl in 3ch-sp, 3 ch] 5 times, 3dc-cl in 3ch-sp, 1 FPdc around next st, slst in top of 3-ch to join. (12 clusters, sts, 6 dc, 6 x 3ch-sp)

Fasten off colour 2.

Round 3: Join colour 3, [3 sc in 3ch-sp, 2 ch, skip 3dc-cl, 1 FPhdc around FPdc, 2 ch, skip 3dc-cl] 6 times, slst in first sc to join. (18 sc, 6 hdc, 12 x 2ch-sp)

Fasten off colour 3. Turn work.

Round 4 (WS): Join colour 1, [hdc in top of 3dc-cl from Round 1, 4 ch] 6 times, slst in first hdc to join. Turn work. (6 hdc, 6 x 4ch-sp)

Round 5 (RS): 1 ch (does not count as st), [5 hdc in 4ch-sp, 1 hdc in next st] 6 times, slst in first hdc to join. (36 hdc)

Round 6: 5 ch (counts as 1 dc, 2ch-sp), 1 dc in same st (first V-st made), skip next st, [V-st in next st, skip next st] 17 times, slst in 3rd ch of beg 5-ch to join. (18 V-sts)

Fasten off colour 1.

Round 7: Join colour 2, 4 sc in every 2ch-sp around, slst in first sc to join. (72 sc)

Fasten off colour 2.

Round 8: Join colour 3, 1 scBLO in last st from 4-sc group aligned with FPhdc from Round 3, [1 FPtr around FPhdc from Round 3, 12 scBLO (do not skip st behind FPtr)] 6 times omitting last sc, slst in first sc to join. (72 sc, 6 tr)

Fasten off colour 3.

Round 9: Join colour 1, [1 FPhdc around FPtr from prev round, skip st behind, 12 scBLO] 6 times, slst in first FPhdc to join. (72 sc, 6 hdc)

Fasten off colour 1.

Round 10: Join colour 2, 3 ch (counts as first dc of 4dc-bobble), complete 4dc-bobble, 12 scBLO, [4dc-bobble in FPhdc, 12 scBLO] 5 times, slst in first 4dc-bobble to join. (6 bobbles, 72 sc)

Fasten off colour 2.

Round 11: Join colour 3, [scBLO in 4dc-bobble, 1 FPhdc around same 4dc-bobble, 12 scBLO] 6 times, slst in first scBLO to join. (78 sc, 6 hdc)

Fasten off colour 3.

Round 12: Join colour 1, *(2tr-cl, 2 ch, 2tr-cl, 2 ch, 2tr-cl) in 3rd st before FPhdc from prev round (corner), 2 ch, skip next 2 sts, 1 dc in FPhdc, 2 ch, skip next 2 sts, 1 hdc in next st, [2 ch, skip next 2 sts, 1 sc in next st] twice, 2 ch, skip next 2 sts, 1 hdc in next st, 2 ch, skip next 2 sts, 1 dc in next st, 2 ch, skip next 2 sts; rep from * 3 more times, slst in first 2tr-cl to join. (8 dc, 8 hdc, 8 sc, 36 x 2ch-sp, 12 x 2tr-cl)

Round 13: 1 ch (does not count as st), 1 FPsc around 2tr-cl, 2 sc in next 2ch-sp, *(1 FPhdc, 2 ch, 1 FPhdc) around next st (corner), [2 sc in next 2ch-sp, 1 FPsc around next st] 8 times, 2 sc in next 2ch-sp; rep from * 3 more times omitting last FPsc and last 2 sc, slst in first FPsc to join. (112 sts, 4 x 2ch-sp corners)

Fasten off colour 1.

Round 14: Join colour 2, *(2 dc, 2 ch, 2 dc) in 2ch-sp corner, 28 dcBLO; rep from * 3 more times, slst in first dc to join. (128 dc, 4 x 2ch-sp corners)

Fasten off colour 2.

Round 15: Join colour 1, *(2 hdc, 2 ch, 2 hdc) in 2ch-sp corner, 32 BPhdc; rep from * 3 more times, slst in first hdc to join. (144 hdc, 4 x 2ch-sp corners)

Fasten off colour 1 and weave in ends.

Round 16: Join colour 3, *(2 dc, 2 ch, 2 dc) in 2ch-sp corner, 1 ch, skip next 2 sts, [1 dc in next st, 1 ch, skip next st] 17 times; rep from * 3 more times, slst in first dc to join. (84 dc, 72 x ch, 4 x 2ch-sp corners)

Fasten off colour 3.

Round 17: Join colour 1, *(1 sc, 2 ch, 1 sc) in 2ch-sp corner, 2 sc, 1 tr in 2nd skipped st from Round 15 working in front of ch-sp from prev round, skip ch-sp behind tr and next st, [2 sc in next ch-sp, skip next st] 16 times, tr in last skipped st from Round 15, skip ch-sp behind tr, 2 sc; rep from * 3 more times, slst in first sc to join. (8 tr, 152 sc, 4 x 2ch-sp corners)

Fasten off colour 1.

Round 18: Join colour 2, *(1 sc, 2 ch, 1 sc) in 2ch-sp corner, 3 scBLO, 4dc-bobble in tr, 8 scBLO, [4dc-bobble in next st, 7 scBLO] 3 times, 4 dc-bobble in next st, 3 scBLO; rep from * 3 more times, slst in first sc to join. (148 sc, 20 bobbles, 4 x 2ch-sp corners)

Fasten off colour 2.

Round 19: Join colour 1, *(1 sc, 2 ch, 1 sc) in 2ch-sp corner, 4 scBLO, 1 FPsc around 4dc-bobble, 8 scBLO, [1 FPsc around 4dc-bobble, 7 scBLO] 3 times, 1 FPsc around last 4dc-bobble, 4 scBLO; rep from * 3 more times, slst in first sc to join. (176 sc, 4 x 2ch-sp corners)

Round 20: *3 sc in 2ch-sp corner, 44 slstBLO; rep from * 3 more times, slst in beg st to join. (176 slsts, 4 x 3-sc corners)

Fasten off and weave in ends.

IRIS

DESIGNER: HATTIE RISDALE

YARN

Paintbox Yarns Cotton DK, light worsted (DK), in foll shades:
Colour 1: Champagne White (403)
Colour 2: Marine Blue (434)
Colour 3: Candyfloss Pink (450)
Colour 4: Washed Teal (433)

HOOK

US size G/6 (4mm) hook

GAUGE (TENSION)

A single motif measures approx 6¾in (17cm) from point to point using a US size G/6 (4mm) hook.

SPECIAL ABBREVIATIONS

4dc-cl, cluster of 4 dc
4tr-cl, cluster of 4 tr

NOTE

In Round 7, first dc after dc3tog is worked in same st as last leg of dc3tog, and first leg of next dc3tog after 3-dc group is worked in same st as last dc of 3-dc group.

PATTERN

Using G/6 hook and colour 1, make a magic ring.

Round 1: 3 ch (counts 1 dc) 11 dc in ring, slst in 3rd ch of beg 3-ch to join. (12 dc)

Fasten off colour 1.

Round 2: Join colour 2 with slst in any sp between two dc, 1 ch (counts as 1 sc), 1 sc in same sp, 2 sc in each sp around, slst in beg 1-ch to join. (24 sc)

Fasten off colour 2.

Round 3: Join colour 3 with slst in any sp between pairs of 2-sc, 2 ch (counts as first part of 4dc-cl), (complete 4dc-cl, 2 ch) in same sp, (4dc-cl, 2 ch) in each sp between pairs of 2-sc around, slst in first ch at top of first 4dc-cl to join. (12 x 4dc-cl, 12 x 2ch-sp)

Fasten off colour 3.

Round 4: Join colour 4 with slst in any 2ch-sp, (4 ch, 4tr-cl, 4 ch, slst) in same sp, *slst into next 2ch-sp, (4 ch, 4tr-cl, 4 ch, slst) in same sp; rep from * around, slst in beg 2-ch sp, slst in beg slst to join. (12 x 4tr-cl)

Fasten off colour 4.

Round 5: Join colour 2 with slst in space between sts in middle of any 4tr-cl, 1 ch (counts as 1 sc), (1 sc, 5 ch) in same sp, *(2 sc, 5 ch) in space between sts in middle of next 4tr-cl; rep from * around, slst in beg 1-ch to join. (24 sc, 12 x 5ch-sp)

Fasten off colour 2.

Round 6: Join colour 1 with slst in any 5ch-sp, 3 ch (counts as 1 dc), 6 dc in same sp, *7 dc in next 5ch-sp; rep from * around, slst in top of beg 3-ch to join, do not fasten off. (84 dc)

Round 7: 3 ch (counts as first part of dc3tog), complete dc3tog over 2nd and 3rd sts, 1 dc in 3rd st, 1 dc in 5th st, dc3tog over 5th, 6th and 7th sts, 2 ch, dc3tog over 8th, 9th and 10th sts, 1 dc in 10th st, 1 dc in 12th st, dc3tog beg in 12th st, 3 ch, [dc3tog, 1 dc in prev dc, 2 dc, dc3tog beg in prev dc, 2 ch, dc3tog, 1 dc in prev dc, 2 dc, dc3tog beg in prev dc, 3 ch] 5 times, slst in top of beg dc3tog to join, do not fasten off. (24 x dc3tog, 36 dc, 6 x 2ch-sp, 6 x 3ch-sp)

Round 8: 2 ch (counts as 1 hdc), 1 hdc in same st, *4 hdc, 2 hdc in 2ch-sp, 4 hdc, 2hdc in next st, (1 hdc, 2 ch, 1 hdc) in 3ch-sp (corner), 2 hdc in next sp; rep from * 5 more times omitting final 2 hdc on last rep, slst in top of beg 2-ch to join. (96 hdc, 6 x 2ch-sp corners)

Fasten off and weave in ends.

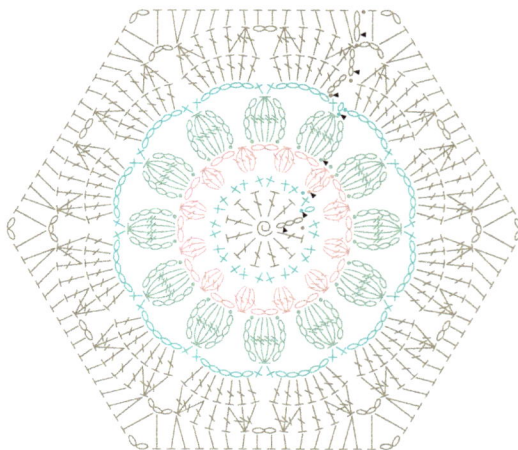

CATALINA

DESIGNER: JULIE YEAGER

YARN

Scheepjes River Washed, sport (4ply), in foll shade:
Colour 1: Danube (948)
Scheepjes Stone Washed, sport (4ply), in foll shades:
Colour 2: Moon Stone (801)
Colour 3: Lemon Quartz (812)

HOOK

US size G/6 (4mm)

GAUGE (TENSION)

A single motif measures approx 8in (20cm) using a US size G/6 (4mm) hook.

SPECIAL ABBREVIATIONS

3tr-cl, cluster of 3 tr
3tr-cl group, ([3tr-cl, 3 ch] twice, 3tr-cl) in same sp
W-st, ([1 dc, 2 ch] twice, 1 dc) in same st or sp

NOTE

In Rounds 4 and 6 space between dc groups is not a ch-sp.

PATTERN

Using G/6 hook and colour 1, 4 ch, slst to join into a ring.

Round 1: 1 ch (does not count as st), 8 sc in ring, slst in first sc to join. (8 sc)

Fasten off colour 1.

Round 2: Join colour 2 with slst in any st, 6 ch (counts as 1 dc, 3 ch), [3tr-cl, 3 ch, 1 dc, 3 ch] 3 times, 3tr-cl, 3 ch, slst in 3rd ch of beg ch-6 to join. (4 dc, 4 x 3tr-cl, 8 x 3ch-sp)

Fasten off colour 2.

Round 3: Join colour 3 with slst in any 3ch-sp, 3 ch (counts as 1 dc throughout), 4 dc in same sp, [5 dc in 3ch-sp] 7 times, slst in top of beg 3-ch to join. (40 dc)

Fasten off colour 3.

Round 4: Join colour 1 with slst in space between 5-dc groups above single dc in Round 2, 5 ch (counts as 1 dc, 2 ch), (1 dc, 2 ch, 1 dc) in same space, [3tr-cl group in next space, W-st in next space] 3 times, 3tr-cl group in next space, slst in 3rd ch of beg 5-ch to join. (4 W-sts, 4 x 3tr-cl groups)

Fasten off colour 1.

Round 5: Join colour 3 with slst in 3ch-sp between first and 2nd cluster of any 3tr-cl group, 3 ch, 5 dc in same sp, *1 ch, 6 dc in next 3ch-sp, [4 dc in 2ch-sp] twice, 6 dc in 3ch-sp; rep from * 3 more times omitting last 6 dc, slst in top of beg 3-ch to join. (80 dc, 4 x 1ch-sp corners)

Fasten off colour 3.

Round 6: Join colour 2 with slst in space between 4-dc group and first 6-dc group of corner, 5 ch (counts as 1 dc, 2 ch), (1 dc, 2 ch, 1 dc) in same space, [1 ch, 3tr-cl group in 1ch-sp, 1 ch, W-st in next space, 1 dc in next space, W-st in next sp] 4 times omitting last W-st, slst in 3rd ch of beg 5-ch to join. (8 W-sts, 4 x 3tr-cl groups, 4 dc, 8 ch)

Fasten off colour 2.

Round 7: Join colour 3 with slst in first 2ch-sp of W-st before corner, 2 ch (counts as 1 hdc), 2 hdc in same sp, *3 hdc in 2ch-sp, 2 dc in 1ch-sp, 4 dc in 3ch-sp, 1 FPtr around post of 3tr-cl, 4 dc in 3ch-sp, 2 dc in 1ch-sp, [3 hdc in 2ch-sp] twice, 1 dc between W-st and dc, 1 dc between dc and next W-st, 3 hdc in 2ch-sp; rep from * 3 more times omitting last 3 hdc, slst in top of beg 2-ch. (48 hdc, 56 dc, 4 FPtr)

Fasten off colour 3.

Round 8: Join colour 1 with slst in any st, 1 sc in each st and 3 sc in each FPtr, slst in beg sc to join. (116 sc)

Fasten off and weave in ends.

LOVE IN A MIST

DESIGNER: CAITIE MOORE

YARN

Nurturing Fibres Eco-Cotton, light
worsted (DK), in foll shades:

Colour 1: Sunglow
Colour 2: Persian
Colour 3: Baltic
Colour 4: Vanilla
Colour 5: Aventurine

HOOK

US size G/6 (4mm) hook

GAUGE (TENSION)

A single motif measures approx
6in (15cm) using a US size G/6
(4mm) hook.

SPECIAL ABBREVIATIONS

croc st, 5 dc bottom to top up post
of first dc, 2ch-picot, 5 dc top to
bottom down post of next dc
2ch-picot, picot with 2 ch
3dc-bobble, bobble of 3 dc, 1 ch

NOTE

*Join yarn with standing sts
unless otherwise indicated, and
join round with invisible join in
standing st.*

PATTERN

Using G/6 hook and colour 1,
make a magic ring.

Round 1: 8 hdc in ring. (8 hdc)

Fasten off colour 1.

Round 2: Join colour 2 in any
st, *(1 sc, 1 ch, 1 dc, 1 ch, 1 sc) in
same st; rep from * to end. (16
sc, 8 dc, 16 ch)

Fasten off colour 2.

Round 3: Join colour 3 in 3rd
loop of hdc from Round 1, 3 dc
in each st around. (24 dc)

Fasten off colour 3.

Round 4: Join colour 4 in any
st, *2 hdc, 2 hdc in same st; rep
from * around. (32 hdc)

Fasten off colour 4.

Round 5: Join colour 5 in any
st, *2 dc, 3 ch, skip 2 sts; rep
from * to end. (16 dc, 8 x 3ch-
sp)

Fasten off colour 5.

Round 6: Join colour 5 to Round 4 in hdc
to right of dc from Round 5, *1 sc, croc st
around 2-dc from Round 5, 1 sc in Round 4;
rep from * to end. (96 sts, 8 picot)

Fasten off colour 5.

Round 7: Join colour 1 in 3ch-sp from
Round 5, *8 dc in 3ch-sp, skip 2 dc; rep
from * to end. (64 dc)

Fasten off colour 1.

Round 8: Join colour 4 in any st, *7 hdc,
2 hdc in same st; rep from * to end. (72 hdc)

Fasten off colour 4.

Round 9: Join colour 4 in any st, 72 FPdc.

Fasten off colour 4.

Round 10: Join colour 4 in any st, 72 FPdc.

ROUNDS 1-6

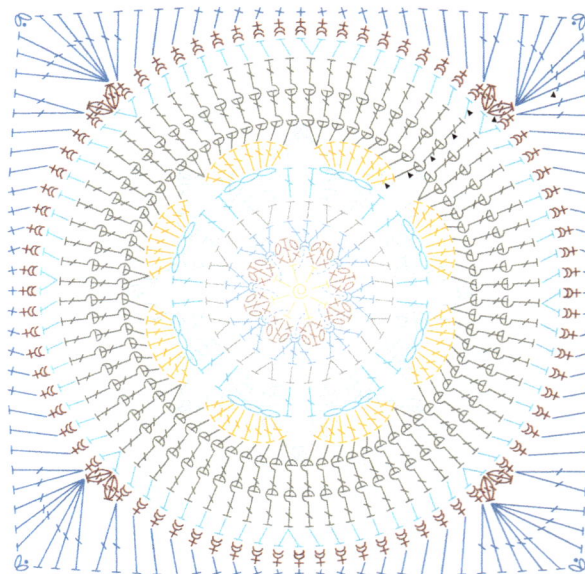

ROUNDS 7-13

Fasten off colour 4.

Round 11: Join colour 5 in any st, *8 hdc, 2 hdc in same st; rep from * to end. (80 hdc)

Fasten off colour 5.

Round 12: Join colour 2 in st aligned with Round 6 petal, *[3dc-bobble] twice in same st, 1 sc in 3rd loop of next 19 hdc; rep from * to end. (76 sc, 8 bobbles)

Fasten off colour 2.

Round 13: Join colour 3 in 1 ch of first 3dc-bobble, *(3 dc, 2ch-picot, 3 dc) in same st, skip bobble, 2 dc in same st, 3 hdc, 11 sc, 3 hdc, 2 dc in same st; rep from * to end. (108 sts, 4 picot corners)

Fasten off and weave in ends.

ROSEMARY CLUSTERS

DESIGNER: JULIE YEAGER

YARN

Scheepjes Stone Washed, sport (4ply), in foll shades:
Colour 1: Pink Quartzite (821)
Colour 3: Coral (816)
Colour 5: Larimar (828)
Colour 7: Malachite (825)
Scheepjes River Washed, sport (4ply), in foll shades:
Colour 2: Nile (944)
Colour 4: Yarra (949)
Colour 6: Ganges (945)

HOOK

US size G/6 (4mm) hook.

GAUGE (TENSION)

A single motif measures approx 8in (20cm) using a US size G/6 (4mm) hook.

SPECIAL ABBREVIATIONS

2dc-cl, cluster of 2 dc
3dc-cl, cluster of 3 dc
spike dc, double crochet worked in st two or more rows below

NOTE

Keep a loose hand with front post trebles and with spike sts.

PATTERN

Using G/6 hook and colour 1, 4 ch, slst to join into a ring.

Round 1: Working into ring, 3 ch, 1 dc in same place to complete first 2dc-cl, [2 ch, 2dc-cl] 7 times, 2 ch, slst in top of first 2dc-cl. (8 x 2dc-cl, 8 x 2ch-sp)

Fasten off colour 1.

Round 2: Join colour 2 with slst in any 2ch-sp, 3 ch (counts as 1 dc throughout), 2 dc in same sp, [1 FPdc around top of next 2dc-cl, 3 dc in 2ch-sp] 8 times omitting last 3 sts, slst in top of beg 3-ch to join. (32 dc)

Fasten off colour 2.

Round 3: Join colour 3 with slst in any FPdc, 3 ch, (counts as first dc of 3dc-cl), complete first 3dc-cl in same st, [3 ch, 3dc-cl] twice in same st for corner, *skip 3 sts, 1 sc, 1 FPtr around top of 2dc-cl in Round 1, 1 sc in same st as prev sc, skip 3 sts, ([3dc-cl, 3 ch] twice, 3dc-cl) in next st for corner; rep from * around omitting last corner, slst in top of first 3dc-cl to join. (12 x 3dc-cl, 8 x 3ch-sp, 4 FPtr, 8 sc)

Fasten off colour 3.

continued on next page >

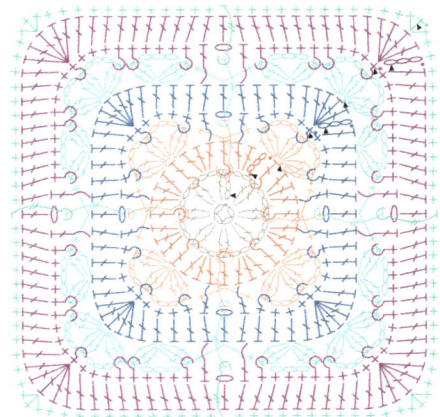

Round 4: Join colour 4 with FPsc around top of middle cluster of any three 3dc-cl group, 3 sc in next 3ch-sp, 1 FPsc around top of next cluster, *spike dc in dc from Round 2, 1 ch, spike dc in dc from Round 2, cont in Round 3, [1 FPsc around top of next 3dc-cl, 3 sc in next 3ch-sp] twice, 1 FPsc around top of next 3dc-cl; rep from * around omitting last 5 sts, slst in first FPsc to join. (44 sts, 4 ch)

Round 5: 3 ch, 4 dc in same st, [5 dc, 1 dc in 1ch-sp, 5 dc, 5 dc in next st] around omitting last 5 sts, slst in top of beg 3-ch to join. (64 dc)

Fasten off colour 4.

Round 6: Join colour 5 with slst in 3rd dc of any 5-dc corner, 3 ch, complete first 3dc-cl in same st, [3 ch, 3dc-cl] twice in same st for corner, *skip 3 sts, (3dc-cl, 3 ch, 3dc-cl) in next st, skip 3 sts, 1 sc, FPtr in FPtr from Round 3, 1 sc in same st as prev sc, skip 3 sts, (3dc-cl, 3 ch, 3dc-cl) in next st, skip 3 sts, ([3dc-cl, 3 ch] twice, 3dc-cl) in next st for corner; rep from * around omitting last corner, slst in first 3dc-cl to join. (28 x 3dc-cl, 16 x 3ch-sp, 8 sc, 4 FPtr)

Fasten off colour 5.

Round 7: Join colour 6 with FPsc around top of middle cluster of any three 3dc-cl groups, *3 sc in next 3ch-sp, FPsc around top of next 2 clusters, 3 sc in next 3ch-sp, FPsc around top of next cluster, spike dc in dc in Round 5, 1 ch, spike dc in dc in Round 5, cont in Round 6, FPsc around top of next 3dc-cl, 3 sc in next 3ch-sp, FPsc around top of next two 3dc-cl, 3 sc in next 3ch-sp, FPsc around top of next 3dc-cl; rep from * around omitting last st, slst in first FPsc to join. (84 sts, 4 ch)

Round 8: 3 ch, 4 dc in same st, [10 dc, 1 dc in 1ch-sp, 10 dc, 5 dc in next st] around omitting last 5 sts, slst in top of beg 3-ch to join. (104 dc)

Fasten off colour 6.

Round 9: Join colour 7 with sc in 3rd dc of any 5-dc corner, 1 sc in same st, *12 sc, 1 FPtr in FPtr in Round 6, skip 1 st, cont in Round 8, 12 sc, 3 sc in next st for corner; rep from * around omitting last 2 sts and ending with 1 sc in same st as beg sc, slst in first st to join. (108 sc, 4 tr)

Fasten off and weave in ends.

OCTAGONAL FLOWER

DESIGNER: LYNNE ROWE

YARN

Ricorumi DK Cotton, light worsted (DK), in foll shades:
Colour 1: Light Blue (033)
Colour 2: Denim (034)
Colour 3: Cream (002)

HOOK

US size E/4 (3.5mm) hook

GAUGE (TENSION)

A single motif measures approx 6½in (16.5cm) side to side using a US size E/4 (3.5mm) hook.

PATTERN

Using E/4 hook and colour 1, make a magic ring.

Round 1 (RS): Working in ring, 3 ch (counts 1 dc throughout), 1 dc, [1 ch, 2 dc] 7 times, 1 ch, slst in top of beg 3-ch to join. (16 dc, 8 ch)

Fasten off colour 1.

Round 2: Join colour 2 in any 1ch-sp, 3 ch, (1 dc, 1 ch, 2 dc) in same sp, *skip next 2 dc, (2 dc, 1 ch, 2 dc) in next 1ch-sp; rep from * 6 more times, skip last 2 dc, slst in top of beg 3-ch to join. (32 dc, 8 ch)

Round 3: Slst in next dc, slst in next 1ch-sp, 4 ch (counts as 1 tr), 6 tr in same sp, *2 ch, skip next 4 dc, 7 tr in next 1ch-sp; rep from * 6 more times, skip last 4 dc, slst in top of beg 4-ch to join. (8 x 7-tr petals, 8 x 2ch-sp)

Fasten off colour 2.

Round 4: Join colour 3 in BLO of first tr of any petal, 1 ch (does not count as st throughout), 1 scBLO in same st, 6 scBLO, 1 dc in sp between groups of 2-dc in Round 2 (working over 2ch-sp of Round 3), *7 scBLO, 1 dc in sp between groups of 2-dc in Round 2 (working over 2ch-sp of Round 3); rep from * 6 more times, slst in first sc to join. (56 scBLO, 8 dc)

Fasten off colour 3.

Round 5: Join colour 1 in middle sc of any petal (4th sc of 7-sc), 1 ch, 1 sc in same st, 2 hdc, 3 dc, 2 hdc, *1 sc, 2 hdc, 3 dc, 2 hdc; rep from * 6 more times, sl st in first sc to join. (64 sts)

Fasten off colour 1.

Round 6: Join colour 3 in any sc, 4 ch (counts as 1 dc, 1 ch), 1 dc in same st, 7 dc, *(1 dc, 1 ch, 1 dc) in sc, 7 dc; rep from * 6 more times, slst in 3rd ch of beg 4-ch to join. (72 dc, 8 x 1ch-sp corners)

Round 7: Slst in 1ch-sp, 4 ch (counts as 1 dc, 1 ch), 1 dc in same st, 9 dc, *(1 dc, 1 ch, 1 dc) in next 1ch-sp, 9 dc; rep from * 6 more times, slst in 3rd of beg 4-ch to join. (88 dc, 8 x 1ch-sp corners)

Fasten off colour 3.

Round 8: Join colour 1 to any 1ch-sp, 1 ch, (1 hdc, 1 ch, 1 hdc) in same 1ch-sp, 11 hdc, *(1 hdc, 1 ch, 1 hdc) in next 1ch-sp, 11 hdc; rep from * 6 more times, slst in 3rd ch of beg 4-ch to join. (104 hdc, 8 x 1ch-sp corners)

Fasten off and weave in ends.

PERSEPHONE

DESIGNER: HATTIE RISDALE

YARN

Paintbox Yarns Cotton DK, light worsted (DK), in foll shades:
Colour 1: Banana Cream (421)
Colour 2: Spearmint Green (426)
Colour 3: Lime Green (429)
Colour 4: Candyfloss Pink (450)

HOOK

US size G/6 (4mm) hook

GAUGE (TENSION)

A single motif measures approx 6⅛in (15.5cm) using a US size G/6 (4mm) hook.

SPECIAL ABBREVIATIONS

2dc-cl, cluster of 2 dc
3tr-cl, cluster of 3 tr
4dc-bobble, bobble of 4 dc
4tr-bobble, bobble of 4 tr

PATTERN

Using G/6 hook and colour 1, make a magic ring.

Round 1: 3 ch (counts as 1 dc), 15 dc in ring, pull on tail to close ring, slst in top of beg 3-ch to join. (16 dc)

continued on next page >

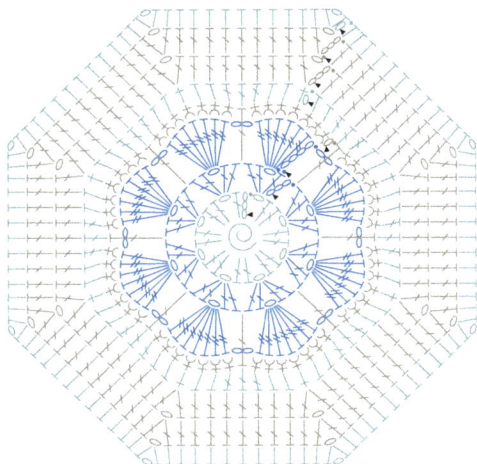

Fasten off colour 1.

Round 2 (bobble): Join colour 2 with slst in any dc, 1 ch (counts as 1 sc), *4dc-bobble in next st, 1 sc in next st; rep from * around omitting final sc, slst in beg 1-ch to join. (8 bobbles, 8 sc)

Fasten off colour 2.

Round 3: Join colour 3 with slst in any sc, 2 ch (counts as first part of 2dc-cl), (complete 2dc-cl, 3 ch, 2dc-cl) in same sp, *(2dc-cl, 3 ch, 2dc-cl) in sc; rep from * around, slst in top of beg cluster to join. (16 x 2dc-cl, 8 x 3-ch)

Fasten off colour 3.

Round 4: Join colour 4 with slst in sp between two sets of (2dc-cl, 3 ch, 2dc-cl), *2 ch, (2 dc, 1 tr, 1 ch, 1 tr, 2 dc, 2 ch) in 3ch-sp, slst in sp between two sets of (2dc-cl, 3 ch, 2dc-cl); rep from * around, slst in beg slst to join. (16 tr, 32 dc, 40 ch)

Fasten off colour 4.

Round 5: Join colour 3 with slst in any 1ch-sp, (7 ch (counts as 1 tr, 3 ch), 3tr-cl, 3 ch, 3tr-cl, 3 ch, 1 tr) in same sp, *(3tr-cl, 2 ch, 1 hdc, 2 ch, 3tr-cl) in next 1 ch sp, (1 tr, 3 ch, 3tr-cl, 3 ch, 3tr-cl, 3 ch, 1 tr) in next sp; rep from * twice more, (3tr-cl, 2 ch, 1 hdc, 2 ch, 3tr-cl) in final sp, slst in 4th ch of beg 7-ch to join. (16 x 3tr-cl, 8 tr, 4 hdc, 8 x 2ch-sp, 12 x 3ch-sp)

Fasten off colour 3.

Round 6 (bobble): Work in colour 4, using colour 2 for bobble. Work over bobble yarn when not using. Join colour 4 with slst in top of 2nd 3tr-cl of any corner group, 2 ch (counts as 1 hdc), 4 hdc in 3ch-sp, join colour 2 with slst in top of tr, 3 ch (counts as first part of 4tr-bobble), complete 4tr-bobble, *1 hdc in next 3tr-cl working over colour 2, 3 hdc in 2ch-sp, pick up colour 2, 4tr-bobble in next hdc, 3 hdc in 2ch-sp, 1 hdc in top of 3tr-cl, 4tr-bobble in next tr, 4 hdc in 3ch-sp, 1 hdc in top of 3tr-cl, (2 dc, 4tr-bobble, 2 dc) in corner, [1 hdc in top of 3tr-cl, 4 hdc in 3ch-sp, 4tr-bobble in next tr]; rep from * 3 times omitting section in [ ] on 3rd rep, slst in top of beg 2-ch, fasten off colour 2 only. (16 bobbles, 72 hdc, 16 dc)

Round 7: 2 ch (counts as 1 hdc), *1 hdc in each st to corner, (2 dc, 2 ch) in top of corner bobble st, 2 dc in next dc; rep from * 3 more times, 1 hdc, slst in top of beg 2-ch to join. (96 hdc, 16 dc, 4 x 2ch-sp corners)

Round 8: 1 ch (counts as 1 sc), *1 sc in each st to corner, (2sc, 2 ch, 2sc) in corner; rep from * 3 more times, 3 sc, slst in beg 1-ch to join. (128 sc, 4 x 2ch-sp corners)

Fasten off and weave in ends.

HESTIA

DESIGNER: HATTIE RISDALE

YARN

Sirdar Happy Cotton DK, light worsted (DK), in foll shades:
Colour 1: Puff (763)
Colour 2: Seaside (784)
Colour 3: Fizz (779)
Colour 4: Tea Time (751)

HOOK

US size G/6 (4mm) hook

GAUGE (TENSION)

A single motif measures approx 5⅛in (13cm) using a US size G/6 (4mm) hook.

SPECIAL ABBREVIATIONS

spike sc, sc worked in st two or more rows below
spike hdc, hdc worked in st two or more rows below
3tr-cl, cluster of 3 tr
5tr-cl, cluster of 5 tr

NOTE

In Rounds 6, 7 and 8 spaces worked into are not ch-sp.

PATTERN

Using G/6 hook and colour 1, make a magic ring.

Round 1: 2 ch (counts 1 hdc throughout), 15 hdc in ring, slst in 2nd ch of beg 2-ch to join. (16 hdc)

Fasten off colour 1.

Round 2: Join colour 2 with slst in top of any st, 1 ch (counts as 1 sc), 1 sc in same sp, *miss 1 st, (2 hdc, 2 ch, 2 hdc) in next st, miss 1 st, 2 sc in next st; rep from * twice more, miss 1 st, (2 hdc, 2 ch, 2 hdc) in next st, slst in beg 1-ch to join. (8 sc, 16 hdc, 4 x 2ch-sp corners)

Fasten off colour 2.

Round 3: Join colour 3 with slst in any 2ch-sp, 3 ch (counts as 1 dc), (2 dc, 2 ch, 3 dc) in same sp, *1 spike sc in hdc in Round 1 in which 2 sc were worked in Round 2, (3 dc, 2 ch, 3 dc) in 2ch-sp; rep from * twice more, 1 spike sc in hdc in Round 1 in which 2 sc were worked in Round 2, slst in 3rd ch of beg 3-ch to join. (24 dc, 4 spike sc, 4 x 2ch-sp corners)

Fasten off colour 3.

Round 4: Join colour 2 with slst in any 2ch-sp, 2 ch, (2 hdc, 2 ch, 3 hdc) in same sp, *slstBLO in next 3 dc, (slst, 4 ch, slst) in "v" of sc, slstBLO in next 3 dc, (3 hdc, 2 ch, 3 hdc) in 2ch-sp; rep from * twice more, slstBLO in next 3 dc, (slst, 4 ch, slst) in "v" of sc, slstBLO in next 3 dc, slst in 2nd ch of beg 2-ch to join. (24 hdc, 24 slstBLO, 4 x 4ch-sp, 8 slst, 4 x 2ch-sp corners)

Fasten off colour 2.

Round 5: Join colour 1 with slst in any 4ch-sp, (2 ch counts as first part of 3dc-cl, complete 3dc-cl, 5tr-cl, 3dc-cl, 4 ch) in same sp,

(3dc-cl, 2 ch, 3dc-cl, 4 ch) in 2ch-sp, *(3dc-cl, 5tr-cl, 3dc-cl, 4 ch) in 4ch-sp, (3dc-cl, 2 ch, 3dc-cl, 4 ch) in 2ch-sp; rep from * twice more, slst in top of beg 3dc-cl to join. (16 x 3dc-cl, 4 x 5tr-cl, 8 x 4ch-sp, 4 x 2ch-sp corners)

Fasten off colour 1.

Round 6: Join colour 3 with slst in any 4ch-sp after a corner, 2 ch, 3 hdc in same sp, 3 hdc in space between 3dc-cl and 5tr-cl, 3 hdc in space between next 5tr-cl and 3dc-cl, 4 hdc in 4ch-sp, (2 dc, 2 ch, 2 dc) in 2ch-sp, *4 hdc in 4ch-sp, 3 hdc in space between 3dc-cl and 5tr-cl, 3 hdc in space between next 5tr-cl and 3dc-cl, 4 hdc in 4ch-sp, (2 dc, 2 ch, 2 dc) in 2ch-sp; rep from * twice more, slst in top of beg 2-ch to join. (56 hdc, 16 dc, 4 x 2ch-sp corners)

Fasten off colour 3.

Round 7: Join colour 2 with slst in any space after 2 dc of corner, 2 ch, 1 hdc in same space, [skip 2 sts, 2 hdc in space] twice, [skip 3 sts, 2 hdc in space] twice, [skip 2 sts, 2 hdc in space] twice, skip 2

sts, (5tr-cl, 2 ch, 5tr-cl) in 2ch-sp, *[skip 2 sts, 2 hdc in next sp] 3 times, [skip 3 sts, 2 hdc in space] twice, [skip 2 sts, 2 hdc in space] twice, skip 2 sts, (5tr-cl, 2 ch, 5tr-cl) in 2ch-sp; rep from * twice more, slst in 2nd ch of beg 2-ch to join. (56 hdc, 8 x 5tr-cl, 4 x 2ch-sp corners)

Fasten off colour 2.

Round 8: Join colour 1 with slst in first space after any corner 5tr-cl, 2 ch (counts as 1 hdc), 1 hdc in same space, [skip 2 sts, 2 hdc in space] twice, skip 2 sts, 1 hdc in next space, skip next st, 2 spike hdc in space between two 3-hdc groups in Round 6, skip next st, 1 hdc in next space, [skip 2 sts, 2 hdc in space] 3 times, *(2 dc, 2 ch, 2 dc) in corner 2ch-sp, 2 hdc in space after 5tr-cl, [skip 2 sts, 2 hdc in space] twice, skip 2 sts, 1 hdc in next space, skip next st, 2 spike hdc in space between two 3-hdc groups in Round 6, skip next st, 1 hdc in next space, [skip 2 sts, 2 hdc in next space] 3 times; rep from * twice more, (2 dc, 2 ch, 2 dc) in 2ch-sp, slst in top of beg 2-ch to join. (64 hdc, 8 spike hdc, 16 dc, 4 x 2ch-sp corners)

Fasten off colour 1.

Round 9: Join colour 4 with slstBLO in any st, 1 ch (counts as 1 sc), 1 scBLO in each st around working (2 sc, 2 ch, 2 sc) in each corner, slst in beg 1-ch to join. (80 scBLO, 16 sc, 4 x 2ch-sp corners)

Fasten off and weave in ends.

CALYPSO

······················

DESIGNER: HATTIE RISDALE

YARN

Phildar Phil Coton 4, light worsted (DK),
in foll shades:
Colour 1: Craie (1937)
Colour 2: Oeillet (1044)
Colour 3: Rosee (1149)
Colour 4: Soleil (1019)
Colour 5: Cyan (1362)
Colour 6: Pomme (1435)
Colour 7: Pistache (1298)

HOOK

US size G/6 (4mm) hook

GAUGE (TENSION)

A single motif measures approx 6⅞in
(17.5cm) using a US size G/6 (4mm)
hook.

SPECIAL ABBREVIATIONS

4dc-cl, cluster of 4 dc
4tr-cl, cluster of 4 tr

PATTERN

Using G/6 hook and colour 1, make
a magic ring.

Round 1: 3 ch (counts as 1 dc), 11 dc
in ring, slst in 3rd of beg 3-ch to
join. (12 dc)

Fasten off colour 1.

Round 2: Join colour 2 with slst
between any two dc, 1 ch (counts
as 1 sc), 1 sc in same sp, 2 sc in
each sp around, slst in beg 1-ch to
join. (24 sc)

Fasten off colour 2.

Round 3: Join colour 3 with slst in
any sp between two 2-sc groups, 2
ch (counts as first part of 4dc-cl),
complete 4dc-cl in same sp, 2 ch,
(4dc-cl, 2 ch) in each sp around,
slst in 2nd of beg 2-ch to join. (12 ×
4dc-cl, 12 × 2ch-sp)

Fasten off colour 3.

Round 4: Join colour 4 with slst
between two dc of Round 1,
crochet a round of slst surface
crochet around dc of Round 1.

Fasten off colour 4.

Round 5: Join colour 5 with slst
between pair of sc in Round 2,
crochet a round of slst surface
crochet around sc of Round 2.

Fasten off colour 5.

Round 6: Join colour 2 with slst in
2ch-sp, 3 ch (counts as first part
of 4tr-cl), (complete 4tr-cl, 4tr-cl,
3 ch) in same sp, (4tr-cl, 4tr-cl, 3
ch) in each 2ch-sp around, sl st in
3rd of beg 3-ch to join. (24 × 4tr-cl,
12 × 3ch-sp)

Fasten off colour 2.

Round 7: Join colour 5 with slst in
any 3ch-sp, 1 ch (counts as 1 sc),
(5 sc, 1 ch) in same sp, (6 sc, 1 ch) in
each sp around, slst in beg 1-ch to
join. (72 sc, 12 ch)

Fasten off colour 5.

Round 8: Join colour 6 with slst
through loops that join two 4tr-
cl of any petal in Round 6, 3 ch
(counts as 1 dc) 2 dc in same sp,
3 hdc in 3ch-sp in Round 6 (over
6-sc in Round 7), 3 dc through
top loops of next petal, (4 tr, 2 ch,
4 tr) at top of next petal (corner),
*3 dc through loops of next petal,
3 hdc in 3ch-sp in Round 6, 3 dc
through loops of next petal, (4 tr, 2
ch, 4 tr) to make corner; rep from
* twice, slst in 3rd of beg 3-ch to
join. (12 hdc, 24 dc, 32 tr, 4 × 2ch-sp
corners)

Fasten off colour 6.

Round 9: Join colour 7 with slst in first tr after 2ch-sp corner, 2 ch (counts as 1 hdc), 1 hdc in each st around and (2 hdc, 2 ch, 2 hdc) in each 2ch-sp corner, slst in 2nd of beg 2-ch to join, do not fasten off. (84 hdc, 4 x 2ch-sp corners)

Round 10: 1 ch (counts as 1 sc), 1 sc in top loops of each st around and (1 sc, 2 ch, 1 sc) in each corner sp, slst in beg 1-ch to join. (92 sc, 4 x 2ch-sp corners)

Fasten off colour 7.

Round 11: Join colour 5 with slst in first sc after any corner group of sts, 2 ch (counts as 1 hdc), 1 hdc in same sp, 2 hdc in every other st along each side working (2 hdc, 1 ch, 2 hdc) at corners, slst in 2nd of beg 2-ch to join. (104 hdc, 4 x 1ch-sp corners)

Fasten off colour 5.

Round 12 (WS): Turn to work on WS, join colour 2 with slst in first sp after corner group, 2 ch (counts as 1 hdc), 1 hdc in same sp, 2 hdc in each sp around working (2 hdc, 1 ch, 2 hdc) in corner 1ch-sps, slst in 2nd of beg 2-ch to join, do not fasten off. (112 hdc, 4 x 1ch-sp corners)

Round 13 (RS): Turn to work on RS, 1 ch (counts as 1 sc), (2 sc, 1 ch, 2 sc) in corner sp, 2 sc in each sp around, 1 sc in beg sp, slst in beg 1-ch to join. (120 sc, 4 x 1ch-sp corners)

Fasten off and weave in ends.

CRYSTAL RIPPLE

DESIGNER: RACHELE CARMONA

YARN

Scheepjes Stone Washed, sport (4ply), in foll shades:
Colour 1: Yellow Jasper (809)
Colour 2: Lepidolite (830)
Colour 3: Lilac Quartz (818)
Colour 4: Amazonite (813)
Colour 5: Turquoise (824)
Colour 6: Moon Stone (801)

HOOK

US size G/6 (4mm) hook

GAUGE (TENSION)

A single motif measures approx 6in (15cm) from flat top to bottom using a US size G/6 (4mm) hook.

SPECIAL ABBREVIATIONS

2tr-cl, cluster of 2 tr
3ch-picot, picot with 3 ch

NOTE

Treble sts in Round 2 make "bobbles" on RS of motif.

PATTERN

Using G/6 hook and colour 1, 3 ch, slst to join into a ring.

Round 1: (1 sc, 1 ch) in ring (counts as first dc throughout), 17 dc in ring, slst in first dc to join. (18 dc)

Fasten off colour 1.

Round 2: Join colour 2 with slst in any dc, (1 sc, 1 tr) in each st around, slst in first sc to join. (18 tr, 18 dc)

Fasten off colour 2.

Round 3: Join colour 3 with slst in any sc, (1 sc, 2 ch) in same st (counts as first tr), complete 2tr-cl in same st, [3 ch, 2tr-cl in next sc] 17 times, 3 ch, slst in 2nd tr to join. (18 x 2tr-cl, 18 x 3ch-sp)

Fasten off colour 3.

Round 4: Join colour 4 with slst in any ch-sp, 3 sc in same sp, [1 sc in 2tr-cl, 3 sc in next sp] 17 times, 1 sc in 2tr-cl, slst in first sc to join. (72 sc)

Round 5: (1 sc, 1 ch) in next st, 2 dc in same st, [1 ch, skip 3 sts, 3 dc in next st) 17 times, 1 ch, slst in first dc to join. (54 dc, 18 ch-sp)

Fasten off colour 4.

continued on next page >

Round 6: Join colour 5 with slst in first sc of Round 5, 1 sc in same st, [1 FPdc in next st, 3ch-picot, 1 sc in next st, 1 ch, 1 sc in next sc] 18 times omitting final sc, slst in first sc to join. (18 FPdc, 18 picot, 36 sc, 18 ch-sp)

Fasten off colour 5.

Round 7: Join colour 6 with slst in any ch-sp, 1 sc in same sp, *[4 ch, sc in next ch-sp] twice, 6 ch, 1 sc in next ch-sp, rep from * 5 times omitting final sc, slst in first sc to join. (18 sc, 12 x 4ch-sp, 6 x 6ch-sp)

Round 8: [5 sc in next two 4ch-sps, 7 sc in next ch-sp] 6 times, slst in first sc to join. (102 sc)

Fasten off and weave in ends.

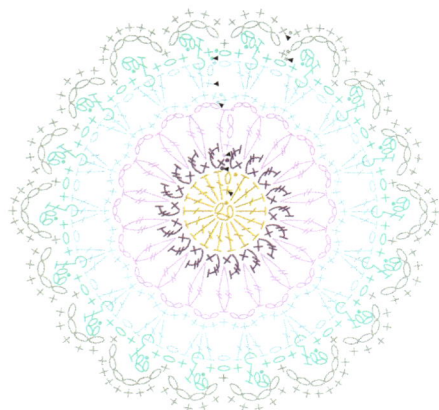

COMPASS ROSE

DESIGNER: JULIE YEAGER

YARN

Scheepjes Stone Washed, sport (4ply), in foll shades:
Colour 1: Beryl (833)
Colour 3: Coral (816)
Colour 4: Turquoise (824)
Colour 5: Yellow Jasper (809)
Scheepjes River Washed, sport (4ply), in foll shade:
Colour 2: Danube (948)

HOOK

US size G/6 (4mm) hook

GAUGE (TENSION)

A single motif measures approx 8in (20cm) using a US size G/6 (4mm) hook.

SPECIAL ABBREVIATION

3tr-cl, cluster of 3 tr

PATTERN

Using G/6 hook and colour 1, 4 ch, slst to join into a ring.

Round 1: Working in ring, 3 ch (counts as tr throughout), complete 3tr-cl in same place, [5 ch, 3tr-cl] 3 times, 5 ch, slst in top of beg 3tr-cl to join. (4 x 3tr-cl, 4 x 5ch-sp)

Fasten off colour 1.

Round 2: Join colour 2 with sc in any 5ch-sp, 2 sc in same sp, [3tr-cl in beg ring, 3 sc in 5ch-sp, 1 FPsc around top of next 3tr-cl, 3 sc in 5ch-sp] 4 times omitting last 3 sc, slst in first sc to join. (28 sc, 4 x 3tr-cl)

Fasten off colour 2.

Round 3: Join colour 3 with sc in any FPsc, 1 sc, [1 hdc, 1 dc, 3 dc in next st (corner), 1 dc, 1 hdc, 3 sc] 4 times omitting last 2 sc, slst in first sc to join. (40 sts)

Fasten off colour 3.

Round 4: Join colour 4 with slst in 2nd dc of any corner, 3 ch, (1 dc, 1 ch, 2 dc) in same st (corner), [9 dc, (2 dc, 1 ch, 2 dc)

in next st for corner] 4 times omitting last corner, slst in top of beg 3-ch to join. (52 dc, 4 x 1ch-sp corners)

Fasten off colour 4.

Round 5: Join colour 5 with sc in 2nd dc of any corner, *3 ch (corner), skip 1 ch, 1 sc, [skip 1 st, 1 ch, 1 sc] 6 times; rep from * 3 times omitting last st, slst in first sc to join. (28 sc, 4 x 3ch-sp corners)

Round 6: [(1 sc, 1 hdc, 1 dc, 1 ch, 1 dc, 1 hdc, 1 sc) in 3ch-sp, 1 sc in 1ch-sp, 7 dc in ch-sp, 1 sc in next two ch-sp, 7 dc in ch-sp, 1 sc in ch-sp] 4 times, slst in first sc to join. (96 sts)

Fasten off colour 5.

Round 7: Join colour 2 with sc in any 1ch-sp corner, 3 ch (corner), 1 sc in same sp, [3 sc, skip 1 st, 3 sc, 3 sc in next st, 3 sc, skip 2 sts, 3 sc, 3 sc in next st, 3 sc, skip 1 st, 3 sc, (1 sc, 3 ch, 1 sc) in 1ch-sp] 4 times omitting last corner, slst in first sc to join. (104 sc, 4 x 3ch-sp corners)

Fasten off colour 2.

Round 8: Join colour 3 with sc in any 3ch-sp corner, 3 ch (corner), 1 sc in same sp, [3 sc, skip 1 st, 4 sc, 3 sc in next st, 3 sc, skip 2 sts, 3 sc, 3 sc in next st, 4 sc, skip 1 st, 3 sc, (1 sc, 3 ch, 1 sc) in 1ch-sp] 4 times omitting last corner, slst in first sc to join. (112 sc, 4 x 3ch-sp corners)

Fasten off colour 3.

Round 9: Join colour 4 with slst in any 3ch-sp, (3 ch, dc, 1 ch, 2 dc) in same sp (corner), [2 dc, dc4tog, 1 hdc, 5 sc, dc4tog, 5 sc, 1 hdc, dc4tog, 2 dc, (2 dc, 1 ch, 2dc) in 3ch-sp] 4 times omitting last corner, slst in top of beg 3-ch to join. (92 sts, 4 x 1ch-sp corners)

Round 10: 3 ch, 1 dc, [(2dc, 1 ch, 2 dc) in 1ch-sp (corner), 5 wdc, 2 hdc, 9 sc, 2 hdc, 5 dc] 4 times omitting last 2 dc, slst in top of beg 3-ch to join. (108 sts, 4 x 1ch-sp corners)

Fasten off and weave in ends.

MANDALITA

DESIGNER: CAITIE MOORE

YARN

Nurturing Fibres Eco-Cotton, light worsted (DK), in foll shades:

Colour 1: Sunglow

Colour 2: Denim

Colour 3: Lime

Colour 4: Vanilla

Colour 5: Aventurine

HOOK

US size G/6 (4mm) hook

GAUGE (TENSION)

A single motif measures approx 5½in (14cm) using a US size G/6 (4mm) hook.

SPECIAL ABBREVIATIONS

2dc-bobble, bobble of 2 dc

4hdc-puff st, puff st of 4 hdc

4dc-PC, popcorn of 4-dc, 1 ch

NOTE

Join yarn with standing sts unless otherwise indicated, and join round with invisible join in standing st.

PATTERN

Using G/6 hook and colour 1, make a magic ring.

Round 1: 8 hdc in ring, pull on tail to close ring. (8 hdc)

Fasten off colour 1.

Round 2: Join colour 2 in any st, *(2dc-bobble, 1 ch, 2dc-bobble, 1 ch) in same st; rep from * to end. (16 bobbles)

Fasten off colour 2.

continued on next page >

Round 3: Join colour 3 in any 1ch-sp, (4hdc-puff st, 1 ch) in each 1ch-sp to end. (16 puffs, 16 ch)

Fasten off colour 3.

Round 4: Join colour 4 in any 1ch-sp, *(1 sc, 1 ch, 1 sc, 1 ch) in 1ch-sp, skip puff and work in next 1ch-sp; rep from * to end. (32 sc, 32 ch)

Fasten off colour 4.

Round 5: Join colour 1 in 1ch-sp above puff st, *(2 sc, 2 ch) in 1ch-sp, skip (1 sc, 1 ch, 1 sc) and work in the next 1ch-sp; rep from * to end. (32 sc, 16 x 2ch-sp)

Fasten off colour 1.

Round 6: Join colour 5 in 2ch-sp, *(1 sc in 2ch-sp, 4dc-PC around 2ch-sp of Round 5 and 1ch-sp of Round 4, 1 sc in 2ch-sp), 1 ch, skip to next 2ch-sp; rep from * to end. (16 PC, 32 sc, 16 ch)

Fasten off colour 5.

Round 7: Join colour 4 in 1ch-sp, *1 hdc, 1 hdc in sc, 1 hdc in 1-ch at back of PC, 1 hdc in sc; rep from * to end. (64 hdc)

Fasten off colour 4.

Round 8: Join colour 1 in hdc above PC, *1 sc, 1 ch, skip 1st; rep from * to end. (32 sc, 32 ch)

Fasten off colour 1.

Round 9: Join colour 4 in 1ch-sp, *3 hdc in 1ch-sp, skip 1 sc, work in next 1ch-sp; rep from * to end. (96 hdc)

Fasten off colour 4.

Round 10: Join colour 2 in 3rd loop of any st, *1 sc in 3rd loop of hdc, skip next hdc, 5 dc in next hdc, skip next hdc, 1 sc in 3rd loop of hdc, skip next hdc, 5 dc in next hdc, skip next hdc, [1 sc in 3rd loop of hdc] twice, 13 slst in 3rd loop, 1 sc in 3rd loop of next hdc; rep from * to end. (52 slst, 40 dc, 20 sc)

Fasten off colour 2.

Round 11: Join colour 3 in sc to right of first 5-dc group, *1 scBLO, 2 BPsc, 2 BPhdc, 1 BPdc, 2 dc in next sc, 1 ch, 2 dc in next dc, 1 BPdc around same dc, 2 BPhdc, 2 BPsc, 1 scBLO, 15 slstBLO; rep from * to end. (124 sts, 4 x 1ch-sp corners)

Fasten off colour 3.

Round 12: Join colour 2 in 1ch-sp, *(2 hdc, 1 ch, 2 hdc) in 1ch-sp, skip next st, [sc2togBLO, 1 scBLO] 9 times, sc2togBLO; rep from * to end. (92 sts, 4 x 1ch-sp corners)

Fasten off and weave in ends.

CLEMATIS

DESIGNER: CATHERINE NORONHA

YARN

Stylecraft Special DK, light worsted (DK), in foll shades:
Colour 1: Mustard (1823)
Colour 2: Cream (1005)
Colour 3: Boysenberry (1828)
Colour 4: Teal (1062)

HOOK

US size E/4 (3.5mm) hook

GAUGE (TENSION)

A single motif measures approx 8in (20cm) from top to bottom using a US size E/4 (3.5mm) hook.

SPECIAL ABBREVIATION

2dc-cl, cluster of 2 dc

NOTES

Motif is worked in tapestry crochet from Round 2 onward.
Change to next colour on last yoh of prev st. Carry unused yarn and crochet over except when you make a FPdc, in which case carry unused yarn across WS (behind FPdc). Make joining slst at end of each round around unused yarn to carry it up for next round.

From Round 2 onward, each round starts with 3 ch, which counts as 1 dc, 1 ch. This is final dc of one side of motif, plus ch to form first corner ch-sp. Other corner ch-sps are formed of 2 ch.

PATTERN

Change colour foll chart.

Using E/4 hook and colour 1, make a magic ring.

Round 1 (RS): Working into ring, 2 ch, 1 dc (counts as 2dc-cl), 1 ch, [2dc-cl, 2 ch] 5 times, slst in beg dc to join. (6 x 2dc-cl, 1 x 1ch-sp corner, 5 x 2ch-sp corners)

Fasten off colour 1.

Round 2: Join colour 2 to any ch-sp, 3 ch (counts as 1 dc, 1 ch throughout), 1 dc in ch-sp, *1 FPdc, (1 dc, 2 ch, 1 dc) in 2ch-sp; rep from * 4 more times, 1 FPdc, slst in 2nd ch of beg 3-ch, slst in ch-sp to join. (18 dc, 1 x 1ch-sp corner, 5 x 2ch-sp corners)

Round 3: 3 ch, 1 dc in ch-sp, *1 dc, 1 FPdc, 1 dc, (1 dc, 2 ch, 1 dc) in 2ch-sp; rep from * 4 more times, 1 dc, 1 FPdc, 1 dc, slst in 2nd ch of beg 3-ch, slst in ch-sp to join. (30 dc, 1 x 1ch-sp corner, 5 x 2ch-sp corners)

Round 4: 3 ch, 1 dc in ch-sp, *2 dc, 1 FPdc, 2 dc, (1 dc, 2 ch, 1 dc) in 2ch-sp; rep from * 4 more times, 2 dc, 1 FPdc, 2 dc, slst in 2nd ch of beg 3-ch, slst in ch-sp to join. (42 dc, 1 x 1ch-sp corner, 5 x 2ch-sp corners)

Round 5: 3 ch, 1 dc in ch-sp, *3 dc, 1 FPdc, 3 dc, (1 dc, 2 ch, 1 dc) in 2ch-sp; rep from * 4 more times, 3 dc, 1 FPdc, 3 dc, slst in 2nd ch of beg 3-ch, slst in ch-sp to join. (54 dc, 1 x 1ch-sp corner, 5 x 2ch-sp corners)

Round 6: 3 ch, 1 dc in ch-sp, *4 dc, 1 FPdc, 4 dc, (1 dc, 2 ch, 1 dc) in 2ch-sp; rep from * 4 more times, 4 dc, 1 FPdc, 4 dc, slst in 2nd ch of beg 3-ch, slst in ch-sp to join. (66 dc, 1 x 1ch-sp corner, 5 x 2ch-sp corners)

Round 7: 3 ch, 1 dc in ch-sp, *5 dc, 1 FPdc, 5 dc, (1 dc, 2 ch, 1 dc) in 2ch-sp; rep from * 4 more times; 5 dc, 1 FPdc, 5 dc, slst in 2nd ch of beg 3-ch, slst in ch-sp. (78 dc, 1 x 1ch-sp corner, 5 x 2ch-sp corners)

Round 8: 3 ch, 1 dc in ch-sp, *13 dc, (1 dc, 2 ch, 1 dc) in 2ch-sp; rep from * 4 more times, 13 dc, slst in 2nd ch of beg 3-ch to join. (90 dc, 1 x 1ch-sp corner, 5 x 2ch-sp corners)

Fasten off and weave in ends.

Chart shows one side of hexagon; it should be repeated six times on each round.

Read chart from bottom to top, right to left.

Each square represents one stitch.

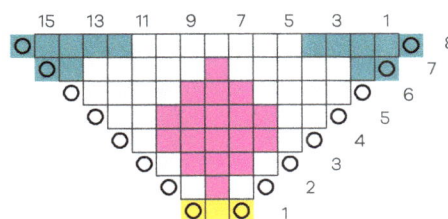

KEY

▨	Colour 1
☐	Colour 2
▨	Colour 3
▨	Colour 4
O	chain (ch)

CROCHET TECHNIQUES

CHAIN (CH)

Make a loop and pull the yarn through to make the first loop on the hook. *Yarn over and pull up a loop; rep from * to make as many chains as stated.

SLIP STITCH (SLST)

Insert the hook in the stitch, yarn over and pull through both stitch and the loop on the hook.

SINGLE CROCHET (SC)

Insert the hook in the stitch, yarn over and pull through the stitch (2 loops on the hook) (1). Yarn over and pull through both loops on the hook (2).

MAGIC RING

With the yarn tail hanging down, make a loop and hold it between two fingers (3). Insert the hook in the loop and pull the yarn through (4), make a chain to secure, then make stitches into the loop (5). When you have finished pull the tail to tighten the loop. Slip stitch in the first stitch to join.

HALF DOUBLE CROCHET (HDC)

Yarn over and insert the hook in the stitch (6). Yarn over and pull up a loop (3 loops on the hook). Yarn over and pull through all 3 loops (7).

DOUBLE CROCHET (DC)

Yarn over and insert the hook in the stitch (8). Yarn over and pull through the stitch (3 loops on the hook) (9). Yarn over and pull through the first 2 loops on the hook (2 loops left on the hook). Yarn over and pull through the last 2 loops.

TREBLE (TR)

Yarn over twice and insert the hook in the stitch (10). Yarn over and pull through the stitch. Yarn over and pull through the first 2 loops on the hook (3 loops left on the hook) (11). Yarn over and pull through the first 2 loops on the hook (2 loops left on the hook). Yarn over again and pull through the remaining loops.

DOUBLE TREBLE (DTR)

Work as treble crochet, but yarn over 3 times before inserting it in the stitch (12). Yarn over and pull through 2 loops each time, until you have 1 loop left on your hook.

SINGLE CROCHET 2 STITCHES TOGETHER (SC2TOG)

Insert the hook in the first stitch, yarn over and pull a loop through the stitch (2 loops on the hook) (13). Insert the hook in the second stitch, yarn over and pull a loop through the stitch (3 loops on the hook) (14). Yarn over and pull through all 3 loops on the hook.

SINGLE CROCHET 3 STITCHES TOGETHER (SC3TOG)

Follow the instructions for sc2tog until there are 3 loops on the hook (14), insert the hook in the third stitch, yarn over and pull a loop through the stitch (4 loops on the hook). Yarn over and pull through all 4 loops on the hook.

DOUBLE CROCHET 2 STITCHES TOGETHER (DC2TOG)

Yarn over and insert the hook in the first stitch. Yarn over and pull a loop through the stitch (3 loops on the hook) (15). Yarn over and pull through the first 2 loops on the hook (2 loops on the hook) (16). Yarn over and insert the hook in the second stitch). Yarn over and pull through the stitch (4 loops on the hook). Yarn over and pull through the first 2 loops on the hook (3 loops on the hook) (17). Yarn over and pull through all 3 loops on the hook (18).

DOUBLE CROCHET 3 STITCHES TOGETHER (DC3TOG)

Follow the instructions for dc2tog until the final yarn over (17), yarn over and insert the hook in the third stitch, yarn over and pull a loop through the stitch (5 loops on the hook), yarn over and pull through the first 2 loops on the hook (4 loops on the hook), yarn over and pull through all loops on the hook.

DOUBLE CROCHET 4 STITCHES TOGETHER (DC4TOG)

Follow the instructions for dc2tog until the final yarn over (17), *yarn over and insert the hook in the third stitch, yarn over and pull a loop through the stitch (5 loops on the hook), yarn over and pull through the first two loops on the hook (4 loops on hook); rep from * in the fourth stitch (5 loops on hook), yarn over and pull through all loops on the hook.

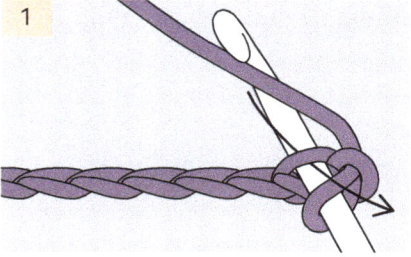

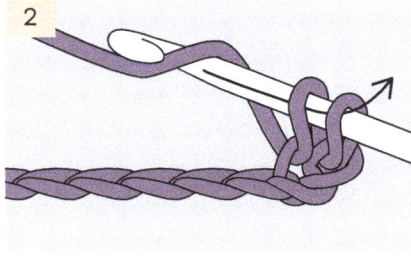

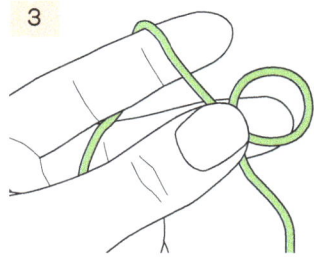

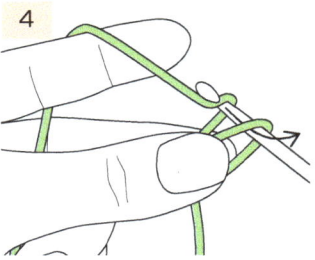

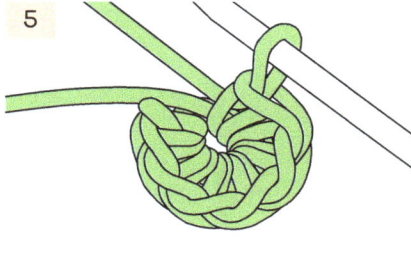

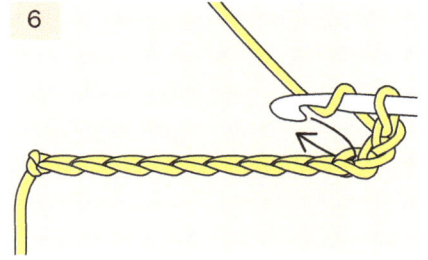

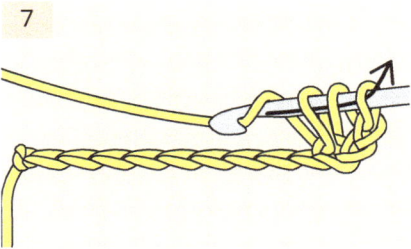

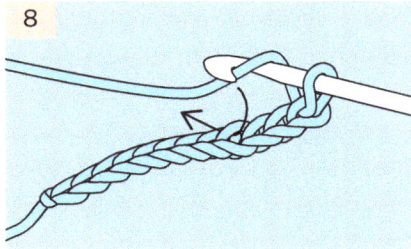

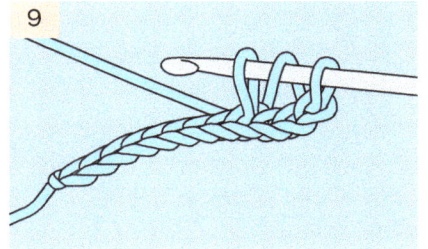

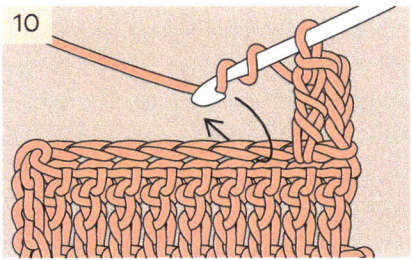

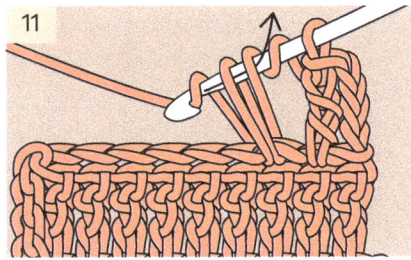

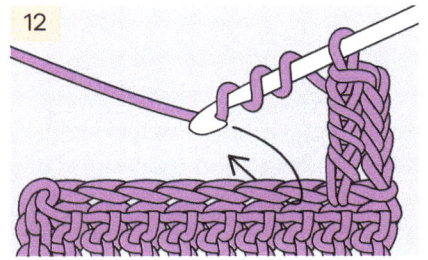

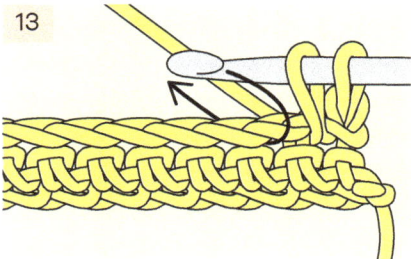

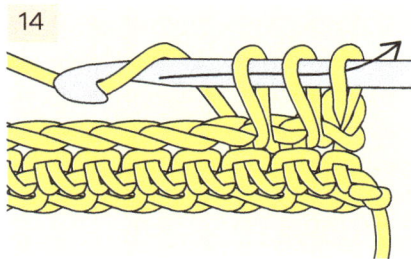

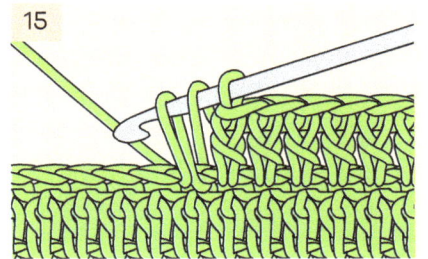

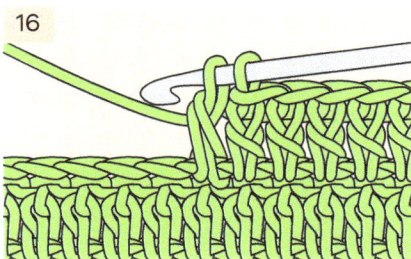

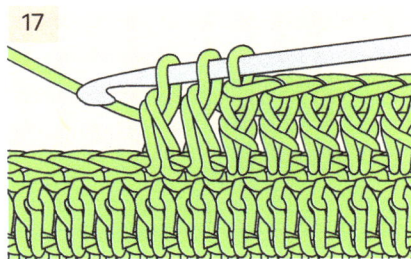

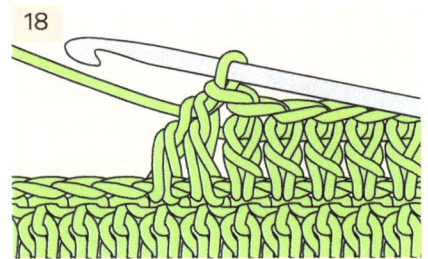

INVISIBLE JOIN

This gives a smooth even edge. Cut the yarn and pull the yarn tail through the last stitch. Thread the yarn tail onto a yarn needle, insert the needle, from front to back, in the next stitch. Now insert the needle back in the same stitch that the yarn tail is coming out of, but in the back loop only, and pull gently (1). Weave the tail end in the wrong side of the fabric and cut the excess (2).

FRONT LOOP ONLY (FLO)

The front loop of a stitch is the loop closest to you. If the pattern says to work in FLO work your stitches in just this front loop.

BACK LOOP ONLY (BLO)

The back loop is the loop furthest away from you. If the pattern says to work in BLO work your stitches in just this back loop.

FRONT POST STITCHES (FP)

Work the stated stitch as normal, but insert the hook from front to back to front around the post of the stitch instead of in it. The illustrations show FPsc: insert the hook from front to back to front around the post of the stitch (3). Yarn over and pull up a loop, yarn over and pull through 2 loops on the hook (4).

BACK POST STITCHES (BP)

Work the stated stitch as normal, but insert the hook from back to front to back around the post of the stitch instead of in it. The illustrations show BPsc: insert the hook from back to front to back around the post of the stitch (5). Yarn over and pull up a loop, yarn over and pull through 2 loops on the hook (6).

POPCORN (PC)

A popcorn consists of complete stitches worked in the same stitch – so for a 3dc-PC work 3 dc and for a 4dc-PC work 4 dc – and then joined at the top. The illustrations show a 5dc-PC: work 5dc in the stitch (7), remove the hook from the last stitch and insert it, from front to back, in the top of the first stitch of the popcorn, then insert the hook back in the loop from the last stitch again (8), yarn over, pull through both loops on the hook. Some popcorns finish with a chain to secure.

PICOT

Make 3 chain (or the number stated), insert the hook from right to left under the front loop and bottom vertical bar of the chain (9), yarn over and pull through all loops on the hook (10).

CLUSTER (CL)

A cluster is made by partly working a number of stitches in the same stitch or chain space, or sometimes over a few stitches, leaving the last yarn over of each stitch on the hook. Then yarn over hook and pull through all loops. It's often worked in a similar way to a bobble, but the cluster sits flat. The illustrations show a 3dc-cl: yarn over hook, *insert the hook in the stitch or space indicated (11), yarn over, pull up a loop, yarn over, pull through the first 2 loops on the hook; rep from * twice more (4 loops on the hook), yarn over hook and pull through all loops on the hook (12).

PUFF STITCH

This is a series of half double crochet stitches worked in one stitch, similar to a bobble but softer and less defined. The illustrations show a 3hdc-puff st: yarn over and insert the hook in the stitch, yarn over and pull up a long loop to the height of the current round or row (13), [yarn over, insert hook in the same stitch, yarn over and pull up a long loop] twice more (14), yarn over and pull through all 7 loops on the hook (15), yarn over and pull through to close the puff. For a 4hdc-puff st work the section in square brackets 3 times then pull through 9 loops on the hook.

BOBBLE

A bobble is made by partly working a number of stitches in one stitch, leaving the last yarn over of each stitch on the hook. Then yarn over and pull through all loops to form a well-defined bump on the surface. The illustrations show a 5dc-bobble: *yarn over, insert the hook in the stitch, yarn over and pull up a loop, yarn over and pull through the first 2 loops on the hook (16); rep from * 4 more times in the same stitch (6 loops on the hook) (17). Yarn over and pull through all 6 loops on the hook (18).

V STITCH (V-ST)

Work (1 dc, 2 ch, 1 dc) all into the same stitch. Can also be worked with 3 ch between the two dc.

SPIKE STITCH

Work the stated stitch as normal, but into the next stitch the number of rows or rounds below as given in the pattern, pulling up the loops to the height of the working row or round to complete the stitch.

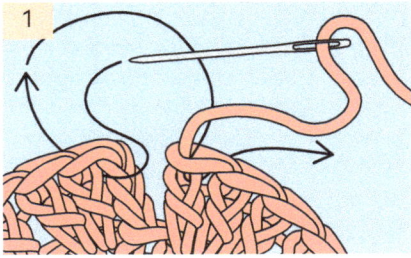

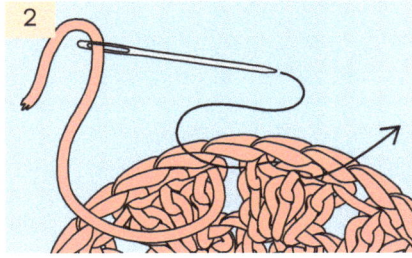

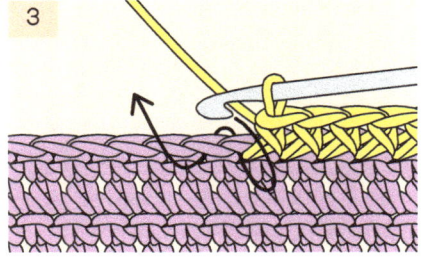

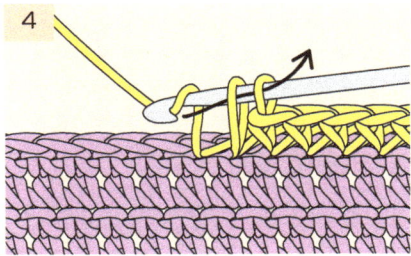

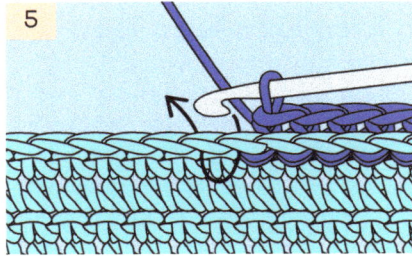

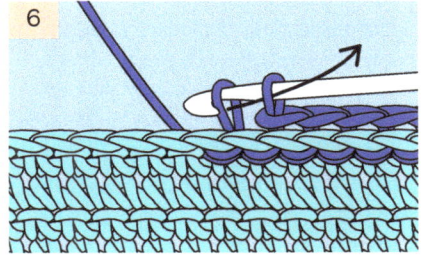

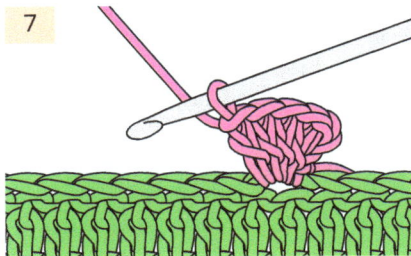

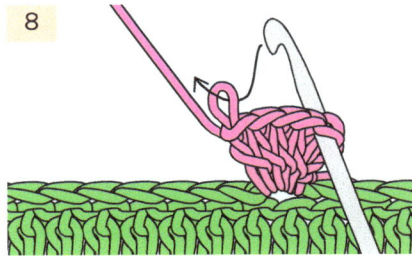

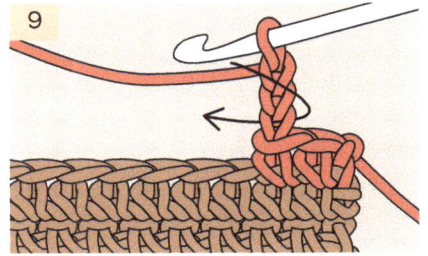

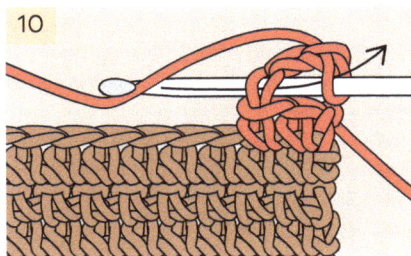

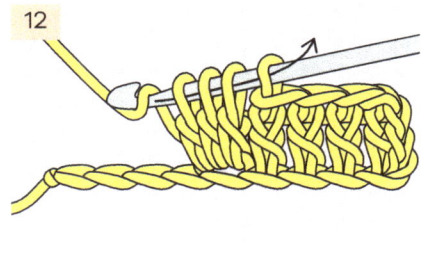

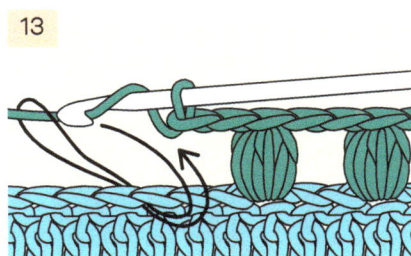

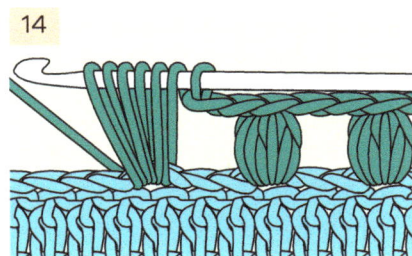

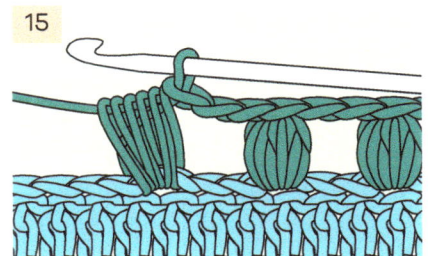

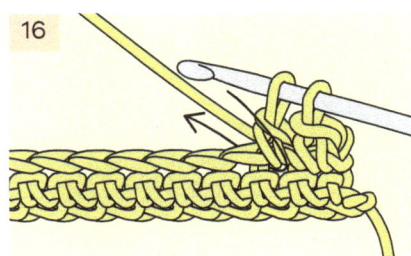

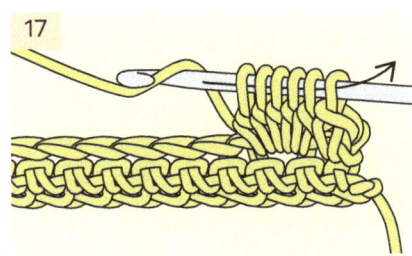

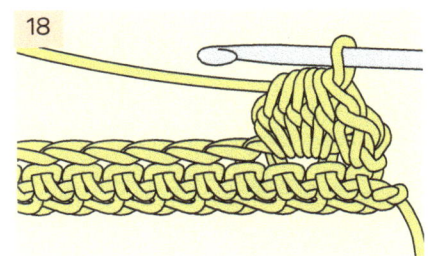

TAPESTRY CROCHET

Tapestry crochet is usually worked following a chart, which gives the colour changes. More than one colour is worked in each row or round, with unused yarns carried along and crocheted over to hide them, so they are ready to use when needed (1). The method of making a colour change is the same in a round or row. Begin the colour change in the prev stitch: in the old colour, make the stitch as usual but, before the final yarn over, bring the old colour to the front (to complete the stitch on the reverse side), then pick up and pull through a loop of the new colour (2). Pass the old colour to the back and continue in the new colour, crocheting over the old colour as you go (3).

BLOCKING

Pin the tile to size using rust-proof pins and steam lightly with an iron. Do not touch the work with the iron but hover over it giving blasts of steam. Leave to dry completely before removing the pins.

JOIN-AS-YOU-GO

With this technique tiles are joined as they are made, which saves time at the end. The general technique is shown on a granny square, but can be adjusted for any square. First, complete one tile (Square 1) and have the next tile (Square 2) complete up to the two last sides of the final round. Crochet along the third edge and make the corner cluster, then 1 chain. Slip stitch in the corner of Square 1 and complete the corner cluster of Square 2 (4), then *slip stitch in the next space between clusters of Square 1. Make the next cluster in Square 2; then rep from * across the side to the corner of Square 2, make the first cluster here, slip stitch in Square 1 as before and complete the corner of Square 2 (5). Continue joining one square at a time. To begin the next row, join the first square as before along one side. Make the next square with one side completed before joining exactly as before, but along two sides (6). The first square of any row only joins on one side. All following squares join on two sides.

SINGLE CROCHET SEAM

Single crochet can be used to create a decorative, sturdy seam on the right side when pieces are placed wrong sides together. Working with right sides together for seaming will make the stitches less obvious. For a single crochet seam, begin at the right-hand edge and join pairs of stitches together through both loops, working single crochet in the usual way (see Single Crochet).

STANDING STITCH

To make your project look a little neater, a standing stitch is a useful way to start a row or round in double crochet, as it removes the need for a slip stitch and ch 1. If you are working with taller stitches, simply make a standing stitch and then ch 1 or 2 to imitate the height of the surrounding stitches. To make the standing stitch, begin with a slip knot on your hook and insert it into the stitch. Yarn over and draw the yarn through the stitch (2 loops on hook), yarn over and draw the yarn through both loops to complete the stitch.

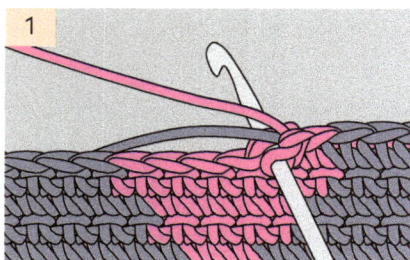

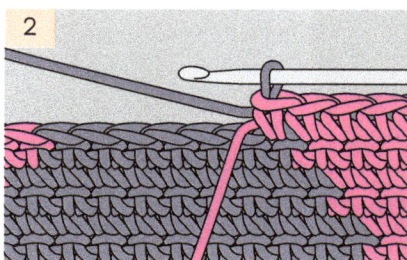

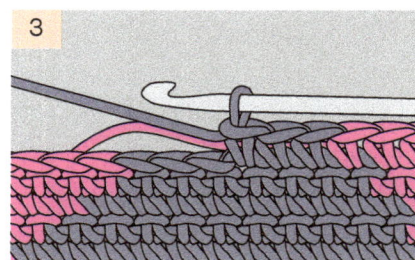

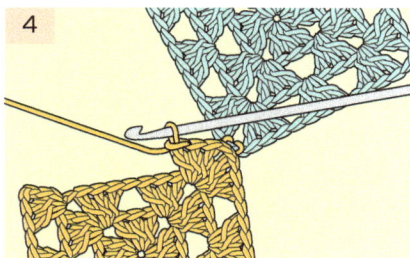

INDEX

THE DESIGNERS

The publisher would like to thank all of the designers whose patterns appear in this book.

CAITIE MOORE
Instagram: @thoresbycottage
www.thoresbycottage.com

LYNNE ROWE
Instagram: @the_woolnest
www.knitcrochetcreate.com

ANA MORAIS SOARES
Instagram: @oneskeinoflove
www.oneskeinoflove.com

RACHELE CARMONA
Instagram: @cypresstextiles
www.cypresstextiles.net

JULIE YEAGER
Instagram: @julieanny_crochet
www.julieyeagerdesigns.com

HATTIE RISDALE
Instagram: @petalshed
www.thepetalshed.uk

ANNA NIKIPIROWICZ
Instagram: @annanikipirowicz
www.moochka.co.uk

CATHERINE NORONHA
Instagram: @catherinecrochets
www.catherinecrochets.com

A DAVID AND CHARLES BOOK
© David and Charles, Ltd 2024

David and Charles is an imprint of David and Charles, Ltd
Suite A, Tourism House, Pynes Hill, Exeter, EX2 5WS

Text and Designs © David and Charles, Ltd 2024
Layout and Photography © David and Charles, Ltd 2024

First published in the UK and USA in 2024
Content previously published in *100 Crochet Tiles* in 2022

The publisher has made every effort to ensure that all the
instructions in the book are accurate and safe, and therefore
cannot accept liability for any resulting injury, damage or loss
to persons or property, however it may arise.

Names of manufacturers and product ranges are provided
for the information of readers, with no intention to infringe
copyright or trademarks.

A catalogue record for this book is available from the
British Library.

ISBN-13: 9781446314616 paperback
ISBN-13: 9781446315088 EPUB
ISBN-13: 9781446315095 PDF

Printed digitally for David and Charles, Ltd

Senior Commissioning Editor: Sarah Callard
Managing Editor: Jeni Chown
Editor: Jessica Cropper
Project Editor: Marie Clayton
Head of Design: Anna Wade
Designers: Blanche Williams and Jess Pearson
Pre-press Designer: Susan Reansbury
Illustrations: Kuo Kang Chen
Photography: Jason Jenkins
Production Manager: Beverley Richardson

David and Charles publishes high-quality books on
a wide range of subjects. For more information visit
www.davidandcharles.com.

Share your makes with us on social media using
#dandcbooks and follow us on Facebook and Instagram by
searching for @dandcbooks.

Layout of the digital edition of this book may vary depending
on reader hardware and display settings.

www.ingramcontent.com/pod-product-compliance
Lightning Source LLC
LaVergne TN
LVHW070058080426
835508LV00032B/3490